WHAT
IF
WE
KNEW US?

ABOUT
KNOWS
GOD
WHAT

CRIS ROGERS

Published by

Lion Hudson Limited

Wilkinson House, Jordan Hill Business Park

Banbury Road, Oxford OX2 8DR, England

www.lionhudson.com

ISBN 978 0 85721 903 9

e-ISBN 978 0 85721 904 6

First edition 2018

Acknowledgments

Unless otherwise stated, Scripture quotations are taken from the Holy Bible, New International Version Anglicised. Copyright © 1979, 1984, 2011 Biblica, formerly International Bible Society. Used by permission of Hodder & Stoughton Ltd, an Hachette UK company. All rights reserved. "NIV" is a registered trademark of Biblica. UK trademark number 1448790.

Scripture quotations marked NLT are taken from the Holy Bible, New Living Translation, copyright © 1996, 2004, 2007 by Tyndale House Foundation. Used by permission of Tyndale House Publishers, Inc., Carol Stream, Illinois 60188. All rights reserved.

Scripture quotations marked NRSV are from The New Revised Standard Version of the Bible copyright © 1989 by the Division of Christian Education of the National Council of Churches in the USA. Used by permission. All Rights Reserved.

Scripture quotations marked KJV are from The Authorized (King James) Version. Rights in the Authorized Version are vested in the Crown. Reproduced by permission of the Crown's patentee, Cambridge University Press.

Scripture quotations marked Message are from The Message. Copyright © by Eugene H. Peterson 1993, 1994, 1995, 1996, 2000, 2001, 2002. Used by permission of NavPress Publishing Group.

A catalogue record for this book is available from the British Library.

Printed and bound in Great Britain by Marston Book Services Ltd, Oxfordshire

CONTENTS

INTRODUCTION

This is a book about us,

    so it's also a book about Him.

    God loves you.

    He is for you.

    He saves you.

    He fights for you.

    He has gifts for you.

    He wants to share His power with you.

    He wants you in the family.

    He wants you to join Him in His work.

    He wants you to stop listening to the lies you believe about yourself and listen to Him.

    This is not a self-help book. If you want one of those, there are many on the shelves of good bookshops. We don't need any more self-help; self-help never really helped anyone. Self-help just helps mask the problems right at the core of who each of us is.

    So this book is about us, but it's more about Him.

    I dread to think what my life would be like if I wasn't following Jesus. My biggest aspiration as a child was to paint eggs and sell them on Whitby Pier. Obviously, if you're an egg-painter, it's a noble career. Many children my age wanted to be spacemen, scientists, firemen, or robot designers. But me, I knew I couldn't ever be that kind of person. I wasn't intelligent in the way schools assess intelligence, which meant I had little aspiration. Egg-painting sounded good to me. I could paint eggs and sell them while sitting some place nice, like the coast, painting the views. I am a creative at heart, which means I knew if nothing else, I could pick up a paintbrush and make something I could sell in order to buy food. If God hadn't dramatically spoken into my life, I would be that guy, painting eggs, with little aspiration.

We all have ideas about ourselves. We believe certain things about our worth, ability, and future. Because of these things, we have drivers – or a lack of them – in our lives. What we think about ourselves will ultimately govern what we do with ourselves.

It is a simple fact that there are more male CEOs in the world than female CEOs. There are more male store managers than female. Men will apply for a job within forty-eight hours of seeing the advert; women will hold back and take longer to decide whether to even apply. Men apply for jobs above their level of ability and are likely to oversell themselves. Women apply for jobs below their level of ability and usually undersell themselves.

We have a generation of women who systemically behave as though they have little to offer. This may sound judgmental of me, but my gut feeling is that there are a lot of women out there who don't realize their ability, availability, and capability.

There are many reasons why I don't wish to explore why men feel they can apply for jobs above their level of ability. What I do want to explore in this book is why we so often undersell ourselves, why we don't believe in ourselves, and why we avoid pushing ourselves forward.

What you know about yourself will govern what you do with yourself. You will hear me say that a lot in this book.

What you know about yourself will govern the choices you make and the way you live.

If we believe we are weak, we will behave weakly.

If we believe we have no gifts, we will not use them.

If we think we have no time, we will not fill it.

If we think we are unable to, we won't.

If we think we don't have the gifts needed for a job, even if we do, we will not apply for it... Well, unless we're men. Statistically speaking.

We have ideas about ourselves that have been created by failed opportunities, broken hearts, and what others say about us. We take others' opinions and allow them to affect our confidence.

If you think you are strong and able and powerful, quick thinking, and able to easily solve problems, then this book is probably not for you. If you're like me and feel as though your confidence has taken a hit, you're not the brightest bulb on the shelf, and you don't have much to offer planet Earth, then this book is for you.

I'm not interested in doing the enthusiastic motivational speaker thing that will pump you up and excite you but give you little that's concrete or of substance. As I have said, this isn't a self-help book. I want to use the pages of this book to tell you some things that are simply true. We have too many people who lie to us, tell us half-truths. What we need is some truth – truth that's going to come from our Father, the One who made us and formed us by His hands.

Hidden to many of us are things that God thinks about you and me. He has not kept them secret, but we certainly haven't heard them and taken note.

This is a book about who God is and who we are. What we think about ourselves governs what we do. If we think we are powerless, then we will behave that way in our daily lives. You are not powerless; in fact, you are the total opposite. You have power that you have no idea even exists or is available to you. We've just got to peel away the lies that have stuck and allow the Father to speak life over us.

Sadly, many branches of the church are not governed by our identity in Christ, but by our failed identity, and we don't even realize.

There is a danger that we believe certain things about ourselves which then stop us from stepping into becoming the person we were saved to be. We are told that in Jesus we are "new creations", but sometimes we still wear the clothing of the old creation.

BUT!

What if we knew what God knows about us?

We all have an identity issue. Some of us do better than others in hiding it. Some of us think we are OK, but we were never meant to be OK; we were meant for much more. Remember what it says in Jeremiah 33:3: "Call to me and I will answer you and tell you great and unsearchable things you do not know."

"Call to me." That's what we want to be doing. Many of us call to the propagated culture to tell us confused and toxic things. But Jeremiah reminds us to call to God to hear wonderful things. He is the only one who can tell us what we really need to know.

Remember Psalm 27:4, which says:

> One thing I ask from the Lord,
>   this only do I seek:
> that I may dwell in the house of the Lord
>   all the days of my life,
> to gaze on the beauty of the Lord
>   and to seek him in his temple.

David wanted to enquire of God in that most holy place. In this book we want to dwell in the house of God and enquire of Him what He knows. We want to seek Him and His way of seeing things.

If we knew who He was and who we were, then we would be able to do far more than we think possible.

In this book, we will look at who God thinks we are and what He thinks we are capable of. If we know what God knows about us, we will do the things He knows we can do.

DIAGNOSING A PROBLEM

Let's take a moment to diagnose a problem. Back at the start of the Bible is a historical event. I call it that because it's not a story. Genesis 1 tells us that we are created in the image of God – historical fact. The Scriptures start with God's work in the world by telling us we were dust and dirt, raw elements, and God took the dust and dirt and starts to form something from nothing. We are made from the dust of the ground. The name *Adam* literally means "dust man". Taking this dust man and dust woman, God breathed life into our lungs and we became living beings.

Get this: God's hands were involved: "We are God's handiwork" (Ephesians 2:10).

We are also told that we were made to a predetermined design. We were made in HIS image. We have to be careful here. When we consider that we were made in His image, we often then read our design back on Him. In other words, we think that because we have a head, two arms, two eyes, a nose, and a mouth, God must have them too. That isn't what it means to be created in God's image. Why would it be important that Jesus came and put on flesh if God were already like us?

To be created in the image of God means much more than looks. When an artist paints someone we might say, when looking at the picture, "Oh, he really CAUGHT their likeness." An artist will capture the essence of someone with their paint and brushes.

It's the same with us. We are made in such a way that we catch something of God. It isn't that we look like Him; rather, our character, desires, hopes, dreams, longings, compassion, and love somehow reflect His essence.

The problem is, from this point on we have allowed someone or something else to form us, rather than the Creator Himself. Remember Genesis 3. The evil one came to challenge Adam and Eve, to tell them there was something wrong, that they should distrust their Creator. So they started listening to a different voice. Because we have done the same, we now have dysfunction in each of us. We end up being driven by fear, failure, and distrust. The world has shaped our thinking about one another, our purpose, and our position. We don't know who we are, so we don't know what to do.

So the world has shaped us from the point of our birth.

We have also allowed church culture and bad theology to shape how we see God and ourselves – bad theology that leaves us feeling we need to earn God's love, prove ourselves to each other, and only find real value in what we do.

The truth is, you are more Christlike than you know.

What is at stake here is monumental and will change the course of history. That's not me being dramatic. If we continue on the trajectory we are on, not only as people but also as Christians, we will end up with a church that is simply not worth keeping going.

What is at stake here is how you relate to yourself, how you are involved in the local church, and how you relate to the world. When we don't know who we are, it slowly robs the church of its full glory. It means the church is full of people who are fearful to be who they have already been made to be. It means the Jesus family is full of people who are mini Christs but don't act like Him because they disbelieve who they are.

The devil is disabling the body of Christ by making us think we are not worthy to be part of it. The alternative is a vision of a church that is neither as diverse nor as powerful as God wants it to be.

The root of this is the devil, who wants to keep us trapped in our own minds, feeling judged for long-gone sin, and telling us we need to know more before we can be who we were created to be.

We end up thinking we praise God because we are now forgiven. We end up thinking it's all about sin. The church becomes a place to manage sin, and therefore we think this is the end of our journey... church.

BUT SO WHAT? We were forgiven not just to be free, but also to be given a place at the table with the Trinity, the family of God.[1] We were forgiven so we would no longer be like our old selves. Remember, if forgiveness was all we needed, there would have been no need for the resurrection. We needed more than to be saved: we needed new life.

Salvation doesn't end at the cross but it begins at the resurrection. That means faith isn't about sin management, but about new life adventure.

Because the devil knows Jesus wants us to be free and available for His kingdom work, he loves to confuse us by

---

1   Russian artist Andrei Rublev painted a beautiful painting in the fifteenth century called *Trinity*. In it the three Persons of the Trinity sit at the table and a space is left at the front of the table. The artist did this to depict the seat that is waiting for you to join.

over-intellectualizing Christianity. If we make it complicated, it must have more value... right? This line of thinking has convinced us we need to fully know it before we can pass it on – so we have an expert mentality and then the unity of the church hangs on how we agree on theology, not on the direction in which we are going. We have been seduced into thinking there is one more thing to learn.

Friends, it's not about being the best taught, but being the most obedient. It's not about being filled up with knowledge, but being filled up by Him: His activity and creativity alive in us.

Because we don't believe this stuff, it has a detrimental effect on the church. Because we believe the lies, we keep returning to thinking that we are sinners, not holy people. We think we need to learn more rather than do the stuff, and we think others have what it takes and we leave it to them, rather than taking what is on offer to us. This will lead the church to being limp, flabby, and inactive, because we are scared.

This is the status quo, and why I believe this book is needed. I believe it's a prophetic book for the church. I want to diagnose a problem and show that the solution is fantastic.

If we carry on where we are going, in ten years the church will have lost ground, lost confidence, lost the respect of the world, and lost the ability to move in the power and authority that has been given to it. In ten years we will have a dead church, or one that is severely lacking in credibility.

But, on the other hand, if we knew who we were and the authority we had, coupled with the power we are given, the church could be the most intoxicating community, breathing life into the most far-gone people and places. If we were to grasp what God knows about us, it would be impossible to determine the future, because the resurrection at work changes what is humanly possible.

If humanity knew who we were, we would not be positioned on the back foot, but would instead be pressing forward with real joy in our hearts. The effect on us in ten years, if we truly knew our identity, would radically explode the church. Our problems wouldn't be about filling our buildings. They would instead be about buildings not being needed because there would simply be too many people for them. The church would have to move back into people's homes to cope with the numbers of those attending.

A STORY ABOUT RABBI AKIVA

I want to tell a story to get us thinking.

One generation after Jesus lived on earth, Rabbi Akiva taught around Galilee and lived in Capernaum, on the shores of Lake Galilee.

Rabbi Akiva was out late one night, walking the shore while meditating on Isaiah 43:

> *"But you are my witnesses, O Israel!" says the*
> *Lord. "You are my servant.*
> *You have been chosen to know me, believe in me,*
> *and understand that I alone am God.*
> *There is no other God –*
> *there never has been, and there never will be.*
> *I, yes I, am the Lord,*
> *and there is no other Savior.*

Isaiah 43:10–11 (NLT)

*As he repeated over and over the line "You are my witnesses"
he became distracted. He approached a fork in the road and
made a wrong turn, and rather than ending up in Capernaum
he ended up at a small Roman fortress. It was dark, and
as Rabbi Akiva approached the gate of the fortress, he was
startled as a voice came out from the darkness.*

"Who are you? What are you doing here?"

In stunned silence, Rabbi Akiva didn't move.

*Again the voice called out, "Who are you? What are you
doing here?"*

*The rabbi called back into the darkness, "What do you get
paid to ask me those questions?"*

*After a stunned silence, the Roman responded, "Three
drachma a week."*

*Rabbi Akiva responded, "I'll pay you double if you stand
outside my house and ask me those same questions every
morning: 'Who are you? What are you doing here?'"*

These are the fundamental questions in the Jewish mind,
and they need to be our fundamental questions too. Who are
you? And what are you doing here? Westerners tend to ask the
question "What's the meaning of life?" We ask this question
and then wonder why we aren't finding the answer within the
pages of the Bible. But the Bible is answering the core and
central questions posed by Easterners: "Who are you?" and
"What are you doing?" Easterners want to know whether their
lives have purpose, not meaning.

What you know about yourself will change how you answer
those questions, and this book will help you explore them.
Keep those two questions in mind as you read on, and we will
come back to that story toward the end of the book.

[I] WHAT WE KNOW GOVERNS WHAT WE DO

Our eyes are not only viewers, but also projectors that are running a second story over the picture we see in front of us all the time. Fear is writing that script and the working title is, "I'll never be enough."[2]

Jim Carrey

2   Jim Carrey's Commencement Address at the 2014 at the Maharishi University of Management (MUM) graduation. Available at **https://www.mum.edu/whats-happening/graduation-2014/full-jim-carrey-address-video-and-transcript** (last visited 27 February 2018).

This chapter will explore the idea of what we think of ourselves and how this stops us from being who God sees us as. Essentially, we have a wonky idea of "Me", which is stopping us from doing what God sees is possible. Often we work from a position of disappointment rather than a position of faith.

THE EAGLE WHO THOUGHT HE WAS A CHICKEN

There is a funny little story I would love to tell you. It's a story about an eagle who didn't know who he was.

There was a boy who had had enough of helping his dad on the chicken farm. The boy was sick of the sight of chickens, so decided he would take his bike and cycle to the top of the cliffs that overlooked the farm. The boy cycled to the top of the cliffs and sat watching the valley below. As the boy looked out, he noticed a tree hanging over the ledge with a nest on the end of a branch. The boy climbed up the tree, looked in the nest, and was amazed to see that it was full of eggs. As he leaned forward, the branch bent, and one of the eggs rolled out of the nest and tumbled down the cliff.

What happened next you might say was a miracle. But in many good stories there is some creative licence. The egg rolled from the nest, bounced off the cliff edge, and miraculously landed in a mound of hay at the chicken farm. The boy climbed down the tree, feeling sad that he caused this to happen.

The egg sat in the hay and was eventually picked up by a farm hand and placed in the chicken coop. One lonely chicken took in the egg and sat on it, even though it was larger than the rest.

The mother hen that sat on the egg was one who hadn't been able to have any of her own chicks. She was the proudest chicken you ever saw, sitting on top of this magnificent egg.

Time passed, and the egg started to hatch, to the amazement of the other chickens. From the egg emerged a scrawny but healthy eaglet. As is the nature of chickens, the mother hen didn't complain or baulk at the young eagle in her home, but raised the majestic bird as one of her own.

So the eagle grew up with the other chicks in the coop, thinking it was one of them. The eagle learnt to do all the things the other chickens did.

It clucked.

It pecked.

It scratched in the dirt for worms.

The bird flapped its wings furiously, trying to fly a few feet in the air before it crashed down to the dust and feathers on the ground.

The eagle believed resolutely and absolutely that it was a chicken. The eagle spent its whole life thinking it was a chicken like the other chickens. He had no mirror to tell him any different.

But one day, late in the eagle's life, he looked up to the sky and happened to see high above his head, soaring majestically and effortlessly on its powerful golden wings, an eagle.

Gazing up, the eagle wondered, "What's that? It's magnificent, with so much power and grace in its wings. It's simply beautiful."

Knowing what he was thinking, a chicken friend of the eagle responded, "That's an eagle; king of the birds. It's a bird of the air... not like us. We're only chickens; we're birds of the earth."

Hearing from his fellow chicken that this beautiful bird was not like them, the eagle continued to peck in the dirt for worms. And so it was that the eagle lived and died a chicken. Because that's all he believed himself to be.

If we believe we are chickens, we will never fly, we will never soar and we will never go on the adventures that eagles go on. If we believe we are chickens, we will stick to what we think we know, follow the crowd, and be nothing else.

The chicken wasn't a chicken. He was an eagle.

You aren't a chicken; you are an eagle. But others in the chicken farm tell you things about yourself: "You're not like that beautiful eagle. You're one of us. Don't try to do anything beyond your pay grade. Don't think too highly about yourself. You are just a chicken."

Do you recognize this to be true in your life?

THE GOSPEL

If we were to now place the gospel alongside this story, it would end differently. Imagine the eagle doesn't finish his life not knowing who he is, but rather, at some point, another eagle lands and invites him to go up the cliff where he encourages him to lean over the edge and jump. The gospel would want to help the eagle re-imagine who he is, encourage him to find his real self, and then invite him to soar.

Jesus doesn't want us to be left as we are; He wants us to become who we should have been. There are too many eagles who die thinking they are chickens.

CAREER ADVISOR

When we were at school we would go to see the career advisor. It was my experience that we would tell them our grades and they would tell us what kind of role in life we could expect. As my friends went in to see the advisor and came out again, a pattern started to emerge. If you were good at maths you would be best suited for a career in finance. If English, you would suit a career in languages. If, like me, you had low grades in most things, the answer was simple...

Join the army.

I don't know how many of my friends were told to join the army.

If I had listened to the poor career advice back at school, my life would have looked very different.

Who is telling you your identity? A career advisor? A relative? A workmate? A friend?

Your Father?

BAD INFORMATION

Have you ever made a decision based on bad information? I almost bought a car that was completely unsuitable because I half believed the car salesman's recommendations.

It's possible and very plausible that we make bad decisions all the time because we receive bad information. Have you ever written someone off and then later found out they weren't as bad as you thought, because of bad information?

Is it possible that you might have written off yourself and your future because of bad information?

The truth is that the devil is a good salesman, and he consistently tells us lies about ourselves. Let's look again at the story of Genesis. The devil gives bad information to Adam and Eve, and convinces them to eat the apple. He claims God isn't as good as they believe Him to be. The devil challenges God's goodness and undermines their whole identity. If they are made in the image of God and this God is a liar, then they aren't who they think they are. If this is the case, they have been created by a being who is seeking to manipulate and control them, so instead they seek to control and manipulate their own future.

Let me tell you some good information about yourself: you are created in the image of God. In Latin this is called the *imago Dei*. All Hebrew words come from a root word or idea. Many Hebrew words come from pictures that were first drawn on walls and later explained with words. The Hebrew word for "image", which is the word used when we are told we are created in the image of God, simply means "image, shadow, likeness". Some people might say an echo; others a snapshot.

You are an echo of the creator God.

You are a snapshot of the divine.

There is something about you that is a reflection of who God is. As we discussed earlier, it isn't that you look like God physically, but that something of your humanity is Godlike. When someone looks at you and interacts with you, they see, smell, or hear something that is an echo of the divine God who made you.

You aren't a mistake; you aren't worthless. You are someone who has something about you that is a reflection of God.

So this begs the question, if we are something like an echo, snapshot, or shadow of God, what is this God like?

This Father God is creative, passionate, loving, and graceful. We have heard about His action in the world and sometimes we get to see His activity even today. Jesus makes the unknown God known through His life. He lived a life of sacrifice, a life where others were front and centre to His being. We see a God who pours Himself out for others, over others, and in others. We see a God who isn't defended by the words of religious people but was defined by something far more life-giving. We see God through the person of the Holy Spirit who shares His power, authority, and activity with us. We see a God who freely gives of Himself into cracked pots.

Through the Trinity we see a God who lives in community and invites us to come and sit with Him at the table to eat.

This is the God of whom we are the *imago Dei*.

Pause.

I want you to pause for a moment and breathe in and out. Let's take a moment to stand up, shake a leg, and give ourselves time to reflect. Perhaps put the kettle on. I have a thought for you to reflect on.

You are made in the image of God. This God is many things, and they are all good.

What has moved you away from seeing and knowing this identity?

What are the destructive things that have told you lies about yourself and have challenged God's goodness within you?

End pause.

The reality is that because of the activity of a broken world and broken lives, we move away from an identity that is God-defined to an identity that is damaged and broken.

Rather than knowing we are eagles, we behave like chickens.

The Bible knows this is exactly how we think, so it offers us a way of thinking that can be really helpful. In his letter to the Corinthians, Paul talks about being new creations rather than old creations. Paul tells us that we are eagles, not chickens.

Paul writes in 2 Corinthians 5:14–17:

> *For Christ's love compels us [moves us forward], because we are convinced that one [Jesus] died for all [yes, even you], and therefore all died [because we give our lives over to Him]. And he died for all, that those who live should no longer live for themselves but for him who died for them and was raised again.*
>
> *So from now on we regard no one from a worldly point of view. Though we once regarded Christ in this way, we do so no longer. Therefore [key word], if anyone is in Christ, the new creation has come: the old has gone, the new is here!*

In other words, Jesus saw we were behaving as dead people, scrabbling around in the dirt. Once in a while we would look up and see the beautiful birds in the sky. But, thinking we were nothing, we kept pecking in the dirt. So He died once and for all, so that our old chicken ways could be gone and the new eagle life might come.

If anyone accepts and is in Jesus, they are a NEW creation. When we read this, "NEW creation", there is a danger that two things might emerge in our minds: first, that everything from our past is bad, and second, that everything about us is bad.

If we are to become NEW creations, this implies that God dislikes what we are and wants us to become something else. Some of us like bits of who we are. In fact, God *loves lots* of who we are. We are created as His snapshot. We aren't all bad. God isn't in the business of throwing everything away, but He is in the business of resurrection. This means He is in the business of bringing back to life all the dead ideas, dead dreams, and dead hopes. To all the areas of your life where people have spoken death over you, Jesus comes to bring resurrection.

In the passage from Corinthians above, there are two Greek words for "new", either of which Paul could have used. The first is *neos* and the second is *kinos*.

Neos is translated as "brand new", like a newborn baby. This kind of new would imply that everything of what was originally there has gone and something 100 per cent new has emerged. You might say I bought a *neos* car. I have a *neos* idea.

But Paul doesn't use this word; he uses *kinos*. *Kinos* is better translated as "renew" or "renewed". The old has gone and there has been a renewing. Resurrection is the process of renewing from death to life. Paul says that because of Jesus' death and resurrection we are no longer our old selves; we are renewed selves.

We believe in a God who wastes nothing.

God takes you and me and He loves us. He looks at us with such fondness, and because of this He is in the business of renewing us. We aren't thrown away so that a new body and soul can be programmed with our personality. Yet our old ways are going and our new ways are coming.

OLD CREATIONS

With all this said, it is possible to be new creations and at the same time still live our lives as old creations. We might know we are eagles but still choose to walk as chickens. We might know we are made for more, made to fly, but we have such a distorted view we remain firmly on the ground.

It is possible to be renewed and yet still live as though we are unrenewed.

I'm a massive science fiction geek. For many years I tried to keep it quiet. But recently people have become aware and I'm able to enjoy publicly what I love.

Recently, I decided to rummage through an old bag of T-shirts I still have and dig out my *Star Wars* shirts. I found one of my favourite T-shirts and I was desperate to wear it as I remembered how it felt so good the last time I wore it. I squeezed myself into the cotton and stood looking in the mirror. It was a great T-shirt. The only problem was, it didn't fit.

It was my old self.

I was a kid when I wore it.

I loved it...

...but it didn't fit. I'd grown up and out of it.

We try to wear the clothes of our old life and then wonder why we aren't getting on very well any more. You might say some things don't fit into place any more.

Because of Jesus, you are a renewed creation, but sadly you can end up wearing the clothing of your old creation and then feel that life isn't going very well.

I often meet people who have come to faith but are trying to keep living their old life. They complain that Jesus isn't making their life better, but they are making bad decisions for themselves. They end up looking to Jesus as the problem while He stands there offering them new garments to wear. We reject them, and Him, because we think we know best.

GOING BACKWARD TO GO FORWARD

Let me share the gospel with you for a moment. You were created for great things. God made you as His beautiful son or daughter, placed you in His garden, and gave you the joy of loving, serving, dressing, and caring for creation. You were made for the task of partnering with Him on planet Earth. But the liar has told you that you are worthless, lacking in potential, and has deceived you concerning the plans God has for you.

We all hear the same lies from the enemy. And so we wonder, we fight, we try to do things under our own steam, we earn what we can to make us feel safe, and we make plans to make us feel secure. But we end up tired, lonely, longing for more, and separated from the One we are made to look like.

So Jesus comes to save us from our sin and our broken old selves. Jesus died a wicked death so we don't need to, and so that we can be saved. Not saved so that we might long and wait for eternity, but saved so that we might get back to the original partnership with God.

The resurrection called us back to Eden: naked, unashamed, and in relationship with our Father.

The gospel means we aren't determined by our past failures but by heaven's resurrection potential. Our new life means we have endless possibilities. Each decision opens up endless hopes and dreams. Our lives in Jesus aren't closing and narrowing our choices; rather, they're opening up our lives, our potential, and our opportunities. The horizon is broadening, big and clear.

A QUESTION FOR YOU

I would love to know how many of us think God tolerates us. I'm not a betting man but I could hedge a bet that many, if not most, of us think that God simply tolerates us. Where would this come from? Why would we think such a thing? I would argue that we think this because we think so little of ourselves. We tolerate ourselves, so why wouldn't He? I would also argue that we think this because the devil is constantly whispering it into our ears. In addition, I would say this because we simply haven't grasped how wonderful the gospel is. If we think the purpose of life is to get to heaven, then we believe Jesus feels sorry for us because we aren't going to make it. So He tolerates us and dies to get us in, even though really He's exasperated with us.

The reality of the full gospel is that Jesus died not only to save us from our sin but also to save us *for* something. This must mean that God sees something bigger in each of us. If God wants to save us so that we can partner with Him on planet Earth before our earthly death, it must mean He sees something others don't. The truth is, at best we tolerate ourselves, but because of God's best, He shows His undying love for each of us. We are forgiven and holy, yet we behave as if we are fallen and hopeless.

Remember John 3:16? Many of us know it off by heart but we still miss something outrageous within it. When we read John 3:16 in our English translations, it goes something like, "For God so loved the world that he gave his one and only Son, that whoever believes in him shall not perish but have eternal life."

This line in the Gospel of John is very memorable. But do you realize that translators have added in one word that's not in the Greek: the word "so". John is writing in Greek, and the word he uses for love is such a radical, sacrificial, and costly love, that simply to say God loves us isn't enough. This love is an over-the-top love. It's a love that looks beyond the obvious value of the object and sees something greater. This love is like a water tap turned on full all the time. This love isn't experienced just once; it's a love that is simply pouring out, over and over and over. The love we have here in the Greek is *agape*. It's one of the most famous Greek words for love, of which there are four types all together.

When the translators tried to translate the Gospel of John into English, they noticed that the powerful dynamics of the original Greek couldn't be easily translated. Because this word for love in the Greek is a dynamic word, they decided to insert "so", in the hope of trying to make the love feel more weighty.

"God loved the world." It feels like a once-upon-a-time love. It happened but no longer happens.

"Go SO loved the world." Now it feels like this love is moving, it's active, it's dynamic. I would love to say it like this:

God soooooooooooooooooooooooooo loved the world that He sent His Son.

Or you could say:

God soooooooooooooooooooooooooo loved _____ [insert your name], that He sent His Son.

God does not tolerate you. He soooooooooooooooooooo loves you. Yesterday, now, and tomorrow. God does not tolerate you today, nor will He tolerate you tomorrow, but He is going to soooooooooo love you that He made sure His son Jesus came for you 2,000 years ago.

We aren't tolerated; we are precious in His sight.

SEVEN WONDERS

As we read through John 3:16 we can notice seven wonders held within it about who this God is who claims to know more about us than we do ourselves. It tells us what He comes to do for us and what we get in conclusion. Let's break it down:

God (**The unfathomable Father**)
So loved the world (**The mightiest motive**)
That He gave His one and only Son (**The greatest gift**)
That whoever (**The widest welcome**)
Believes in Him (**The easiest escape**)
Shall not perish (**The divine deliverance**)
But have eternal life (**The priceless possession, starting today**)

Let's take stock for a moment.
You think you're a chicken.
You're not; you're an eagle.
You are created in the image of your Creator.
God wants to be reconnected with us,
not because we are good, but because we are dead.
Jesus died not just to save us from our sin but for something bigger: for life.
God does not tolerate you; He recklessly loves you.

THE MONKEY'S IDENTITY

Let's take a moment to think further about identity. I want to do this by telling another story. I like a good story, and this one is true.[3]

Around sixty-five years ago there was a little girl in a remote South American village playing outside her home. She was only five years old and remembers very little about that time. While she was playing, a group of men entered the area and kidnapped the little girl. They put a bag over her head and took her without her parents knowing, and led her away from home. The little girl was taken by the group of men and led into the jungle. The little girl doesn't know why, but the kidnappers abandoned her under a tree in the Colombian jungle. At the age of five, the girl was left by herself, under a tree, with no one to fend for her.

As she sat there, waiting for someone to come and get her, a group of capuchin monkeys approached. They prodded her and pushed her. They hadn't seen anything like this girl before. They hit her and pulled her. Eventually, the monkeys walked away, leaving the girl traumatized.

The girl waited, and no one came for her. She watched the monkeys and decided to follow them. The monkeys welcomed the girl. They let her live with them, and they protected the girl and fed her.

The little girl learnt to be a monkey. She ended up eating monkey food, sleeping in a tree, and learning to swing like a monkey. She forgot how to speak, learnt the noises the monkeys made, and started to communicate as a monkey.

This little girl effectively became a monkey. She lived with the monkeys and lived as a monkey. She became one with the

---

3   Marina Chapman, *The Girl With No Name: The Incredible True Story of a Child Raised by Monkeys* (Mainstream Publishing, 2013).

jungle.

After she had been living in the jungle for around five years, the little girl looked down one day and spotted an object on the jungle floor. She climbed down the tree and picked up the object. It wasn't an object that had a place in the jungle. In her hands she held a mirror. Looking into the mirror, the monkey girl saw a human girl looking back. She looked deep into the mirror and saw someone looking back who didn't look like the other monkeys. She took the mirror and climbed back up the tree. This moment was significant for her. She realized there was something different about her. She wasn't a monkey, but what was she?

Sometime later, the girl saw a group of men walking through the jungle. She looked at them and realized they looked like the reflection she had seen of herself in the mirror. The hunters saw the girl and forcefully removed her from the jungle.

Marina Chapman, as she is known today, is now in her sixties and lives in Bradford with her family.

Why would I tell you such a weird story?

We live in the jungle. Life is like a jungle each day as we navigate it. But you weren't born to be of the jungle. You were made to be more than a monkey. It took a mirror for Marina to realize who she really was.

In his letter, James writes, "Anyone who listens to the word [the Bible] but does not do what it says is like someone who looks at his face in a mirror and, after looking at himself, goes away and immediately forgets what he looks like" (James 1:23–24).

Marina looked into the mirror and realized who she was. God invites us to do the same. We think we know our identity, but He holds the mirror of the Scriptures, the mirror that reflects our true identity, to us, and for the first time we start to see who we are.

The jungle will attempt to tell you your worth, identity, and ability. There is no benefit in listening to the jungle. The jungle wants to keep you in the jungle. But we look into the mirror and see a new reflection that tells us the truth of who we are, and Jesus comes as the One to remove us from the jungle so that we can enter into the new world He is showing us.

This book is about holding a mirror up for each of us. We live in the jungle, and the mirror of God's word wishes to reflect to each of us this renewed, *kinos*, identity.

GOD IMAGE IDENTITY

Our identity is determined by the way we view and think about ourselves in the context we are in. It's about our purpose and passions, our perceived significance, and our relationships. We get our identity from those we care about and who interact with us.

We will think we are worthless, giftless, and insignificant when we take our identity from the jungle. The jungle has no desire to help us leave it. It likes us to be there and wishes to keep us. We think the jungle is where we find our true identity. So we believe that we are insignificant and see that we are surrounded by broken relationships. Very quickly, this view allows us to create the ideas and direction that determine what we do with our lives.

Many in the jungle think they are mediocre in terms of gifting, mediocre in terms of worth, and surrounded by mediocre relationships. So the idea that we are mediocre perpetuates. Because of this, we make mediocre decisions; we think we aren't worth any more, and so we become trapped in the mediocre world.

It is all of this I want to challenge.

As you look into the mirror, the mirror is offering you a new narrative. The mirror is Scripture, and the mirror is the resurrected Jesus.

Take off your old self.

Take off your old ways of thinking.

Take off your old patterns of jungle behaviour and allow them to be renewed by resurrection.

Then walk away from the jungle, in the opposite direction, and live as a new creation by putting on your new identity in Christ Jesus.

Stop wearing your old self; it no longer fits. You look ridiculous; it's too tight.

QUESTION

Where is your identity coming from? Is it coming from our source, Jesus? Or is it coming from the jungle and its inhabitants?

My point is this: what we kneel before, we get our identity from. Is your identity coming from the wrong place? Are you kneeling before the wrong things? Some kneel before work; for some, it's the desire for a specific way of life; for others, it's a particular relationship.

THEREFORE

I want us to head back to 2 Corinthians 5 for a moment. At the heart of being a new creation are a purpose and partnership that are important to note. Remember, what we believe about ourselves will govern what we do. We are renewed creations because of the resurrection. The purpose of this new creation is that we become someone new, with new abilities and characteristics.

In 2 Corinthians 5:20–21 we read, "We are therefore Christ's ambassadors, as though God were making his appeal through us. We implore you on Christ's behalf: be reconciled [reconnected] to God. God made him who had no sin [Jesus] to be sin for us, so that in him we might become the righteousness of God."

As renewed creations we are therefore Christ's ambassadors. As Paul puts it, we are ambassadors in such a way that it's almost as if Jesus is doing the work and saying the words, not us.

We don't really talk about ambassadors any more. I'm not sure I've met one in recent years or seen one at work. So what is an ambassador? Being an ambassador is more than being a representative of a particular state; it's more about being the embodiment of the nation. A British ambassador, therefore, is sent to make and enforce the will of Britain in that new place. The ambassador is sent out by the ruling body not just to represent but also to have full authority to enforce what is needed.

Let me put it as strongly as this: what does God know about you? He knows that through Christ you are a new creation: you are now a new you. You are now His representative, sent from His kingdom to this jungle. So when you open your mouth and heart, you are doing so as Him. You aren't just with Him and in Him, but He is in you. Therefore you speak for Him, you act for Him, and you serve like Him. The truth is, we are all ambassadors of something. The question is, will we be ambassadors of HIM?

HEADING SOMEWHERE

So we are heading somewhere. This book has a flow and a purpose to it. As we go forward, willing to accept that there is more for us, there are some new identities to unpack, there are some new powers to understand, and there is an authority to receive.

So where is it we are going? The core of many of our identity issues is that we simply don't know who we are. We are therefore going to examine our position as sons and daughters. We are going to look at the power God knows we have, and then we will explore the authority we have been given.

OUR RESPONSE

How do we respond? Are we willing to see ourselves as He sees us? Or are we going to keep wearing our old selves? Are we going to keep waking up and putting on the old garments, or will we realize we have a new wardrobe to put on? There is so much at stake here if we get this wrong. If we don't realize who we are, we will live the rest of our lives trying to earn and obtain approval from the One who already approves. We will waste years doing what does not need to be done.

SOMETHING TO DO

I want to invite you to go and find yourself an old T-shirt or other item of clothing that no longer fits you. (I am not wanting to cause further issues around weight gain for us here. The point isn't: look, you got fat.) I want you to put the item on and stand in front of the mirror. I'm hoping it's tight, too short, and clingy. When we try wearing our old selves, it just looks wrong. Almost comical, if not ridiculous.

Look at the mirror and realize that you may still be wearing your old self. I want to encourage you to prayerfully remove the clothing, asking God to reclothe you in your new self.

PRAYER

Loving Lord,

You are clothed with splendour and majesty.

I stand here with the desire to live for You and Your glory.

I do not wish to be clothed in my old ways.

Clothe me with the garment of Your glory.

May You make Your light surround me and the darkness disappear from my life.

May I now be clothed in my new self.

May I only know what You know about me.

Enable me to shine for You.

In Your glorious name.

Amen.

You can keep thinking you're coal, but the coal is capable of being a diamond of great value and worth.

[2]
WE ARE SONS
AND DAUGHTERS

This chapter is about your purpose and significance. We are going to look at one of the core identity issues we all have and then look again at ourselves through the eyes of the gospel. You aren't who you think you are, and in this chapter we will explore what this means and the significance it has for each and every one of us.

My name is Cris Rogers. My name is significant because it tells me who I am. My identity is found in my name. As I grew up, my mum would regularly say to me, "You're a Rogers: act like it." My identity as a Rogers feeds how I think about myself; my origin links to my purpose and my significance. When we know who we are, we know how to act, where we belong, and where we are going.

I would go to friends' houses, and before I went my mum would tell me, "When you're at that house remember you're a Rogers." In other words, don't act like they act; act like WE act. My upbringing taught me that Rogerses:

Don't buy on credit; they buy with the money they have saved.
Live within their means.
Don't speak badly of people in public.
Look out for those on the edge and those in need.
Stick together even when things get tough.
Always tell the truth.
Honour their grandparents.
Aren't destructive people, but constructive problem-solvers.
Say, "Not a problem."

I am a Rogers. Because of my family, I know who I am and how I act. I play my part in the world as a member of this Rogers tribe, and now, as a dad myself, I get to help new members of the family become Rogerses too. Not simply in title, but also in nature.

And this is key. I want my children to be Rogerses even when they get married and perhaps change their names. Even when they lose the name Rogers, I still want them to be Rogerses in nature.

To see ourselves as part of something bigger creates identity, purpose, significance. Not just as an idea, but as a nature-changing thing.

ORPHANS

Sadly, many of us don't feel that we are a part of such a family. Some of us don't have a family name we can cling to, or our family name isn't a positive one. It's worth me adding that even members of the Rogers tribe or any other secure family are orphans without Christ.

I know someone whose family name is associated with a number of historic crimes in East London. The name is also associated with bringing down a major well-known crime group on this side of the city. When I first met Frank (name changed), he only introduced himself as Frank. Two years passed before I learnt his surname and discovered his link to this history in East London. His name isn't one he wants to hold on to, and the history isn't one he wishes to perpetuate. I get that.

I understand that many of us don't know who we are.

And this is my point.

John 14:18 reads, "I will not leave you as orphans; I will come to you."

I will not "leave you as orphans".

In other words, we are orphans, but He isn't going to leave

us that way.

So what is an orphan? An orphan is someone whose parents are dead, have abandoned them permanently, or rejected them. An orphan is someone who has been separated from their family and now lives by their own means or is reliant upon the means of someone else.

What if the whole of humanity are orphans? Could we have orphaned ourselves by our rejection of our Father? As I look at humanity, I see a people who behave as if we have been abandoned... orphaned.

Orphans often behave as though they are on their own, even when they aren't. They have an "every orphan for themselves" mentality. It's a world where you fight for yourself, because no one else will fight for you. Orphans often become hardened to others by self-protection. They can be distrustful.

I was in Liberia in December 2015 when I met a group of young lads who had recently been orphaned. I noticed a few things about them. They would grab hold of anything they could get their hands on and not let go. They were pushy and protective. They would fight for anything they could gain and would protect themselves with force.

To live each day as an orphan is to feel entirely alone in the world. Orphans will feel that the world is not dependable, secure, or safe. They will believe that they have few or no bonds with other people who can be depended on at any deep level.

There is an idea that orphans end up with a complex which leaves them thinking that they are the sole person they can trust. Remember, what we think we know will govern what we do. If a person at their core feels let down, this will affect how they see the world and their part in it.

Orphan complex is exactly this. Orphan complex is a way of thinking and coping in a world that a person believes isn't on their side. Counsellors talk about this in terms of orphan behaviours. These behaviour patterns can be listed something like this.

Orphans will often:

1. Hoard possessions, time, powerful positions, relationships with others.
2. Wish they had more, be greedy, and be envious of others and what they have.
3. Fight for their rights, believing no one else really understands.
4. Be fearful of the wrath of an authority figure and see them as harsh and cruel, while also feeling neglected and rejected by them.
5. Be defensive of themselves and feel challenged when there is no challenge. They also struggle to receive criticism, seeing it as a threat.
6. Feel like they are on the outside looking in.
7. Be confused about identity and roots.
8. Feel worried about the future.
9. Be performance-driven because they find their value in their performance.
10. Feel lonely and isolated.
11. Be critical of the loved children they see around them.

    They also tend to struggle to understand why parents want to spend time with their children.
12. Feel unworthy to ask for anything and then be angry because someone doesn't offer help.
13. Have difficulty receiving and giving love.

As I look at this list of orphan behaviours, my soul reaction is that that sounds like humanity! We have all gone through the experience of being orphaned. We can easily look at this list and see these things in others, but I have to be honest and say that I see them in myself as well. I come from a very secure family, but I am still human, and humanity is systemically broken. We are riddled with sin; we have told ourselves we have an absent Father who does not care for us. Because of this, we end up with systemic orphan behaviours in humanity.

WE ARE ALL ORPHANS

We are indeed all orphans. We have rejected our Father and turned our back on Him. We have gone our own way, claiming we can do it alone. We have looked to science and politics to build society. We have built a monetary and consumerist society to feed our need for stuff. We hoard what we have, fight for more, and then complain that we have little. We end up feeling rejected and unloved, so we start to look in the wrong places for love. We become addicted to porn to feed our longing for intimacy and to mask our rejection issues. Shopping feeds our need to feel "normal" and in control. We criticize others to make ourselves feel better than them, and surround ourselves with people who agree with us to make ourselves feel that we are right. We consume social media to mask the loneliness, and we reject friends when they stop giving us what we need.

We are orphans, and humanity behaves as such.

TEMPLE TO THE LIVING GOD

Fortunately, this isn't the end of the story. It's not the case that we are orphans and must behave as such. There is another part to the story: it's called the "good news". Paul, writing to the Corinthians, understood this. Corinth was known for its party culture. People were longing for purpose, spiritual enlightenment, and the feeling of being ecstatic, free, and liberated. The phrase "to party like a Corinthian" was used at that time.

So Paul writes to a group of people who are embodying this orphan behaviour. 2 Corinthians 6:16–18 reads:

> For we are the temple of the living God. As God has said:
> "I will live with them
>   and walk among them,
> and I will be their God,
>   and they will be my people."
> Therefore,
> "Come out from them
>   and be separate,
>   says the Lord.
> Touch no unclean thing,
>   and I will receive you."
>
> And,
> "I will be a Father to you,
>   and you will be my sons and daughters,
>   says the Lord Almighty."

"I will be a Father to you, and you will be my sons and daughters."

This is significant. We rejected Him, but still the Father does not reject us. We will be to Him as if we were His own flesh and blood.

CULTURE

We live in an age where the family structure is fractured and broken. We live in a culture damaged by broken relationships. We live in a world where fathers are jerks, idiots, fools, and losers. Some are oppressive and some are absent from family life. Many wives are abused physically and emotionally. Sons raise themselves into adult life on a diet of pornography, online media, and YouTube videos. Sadly, daughters see their fathers and think that's all they too are worth, and walk the same path as their mothers. So when we hear we have a heavenly Father, we shrug and don't believe He can be better than the rest.

But this Father has no representation in our culture. Yet our culture has stolen from Him and distorted our understanding of Him. Jesus tells us, "Anyone who has seen me has seen the Father" (John 14:9). As we read the Scriptures, we come to realize that our Father, our Abba, our Daddy, is compassionate and kind, slow to anger, and quick to love. He isn't an absent father but a tender presence. So what we find in this language of sonship and daughtership is a powerful antidote to a deadly poison, not a sticking plaster that masks the hurt.

THE STORY... THE START

Let's go back to the same passage we looked at in the last chapter. Genesis 1:27 reads, "So God created humankind in his image, in the image of God he created them; male and female he created them" (NRSVA).

The start of the Genesis story is one of creation and fathering. Adam and Eve are fathered by God in His own image. Adam and Eve's creation is after their Father's likeness. Not only are they in His likeness, but they are also given responsibility for what He is responsible for. So it seems that his fathering is about more than just making mini versions of Himself: it is about extending His power and responsibility.

So what is extended to Adam and Eve?

They are given the position of **representing their Father** as vice-regents over creation itself (Genesis 1:26–28).

They are given the **privilege of intimacy with their Father** (Genesis 3:8) and of reflecting back to Him His glory.

They are positioned as **partners with Him in creating** (Genesis 2:15).

LIKE FATHER, LIKE SON

Right from the start, the pattern is laid down for Adam and Eve: like Father, like son. As God ruled over creation, so the sons and daughters were to represent and embody that rule.

We were created and fathered to be sons and daughters.

Sadly, we orphaned ourselves. We decided we didn't need to represent our Father and chose to be our own regents and rulers. We didn't need intimacy; we could be intimate with ourselves. We didn't need any partnership because we could do it alone.

We separated ourselves.

We orphaned ourselves.

We left ourselves alone.

OUR IDENTITY IS NOT DETERMINED BY OUR CIRCUMSTANCES

The year 2016 saw many things happen in the news: an above average number of celebrities died, the multiple conflicts in the Middle East continued, children and widows were let down as they became displaced refugees trapped in borderlands, and Donald Trump was elected President of the USA. The year 2016 will always be remembered as an odd one.

But during 2016 there was also some news that, strangely, had a wonderful buzz about it. The news broke that Archbishop Justin Welby's father was not his real father. The media thought they had discovered something that would challenge the Archbishop's identity and position. Surely an illegitimate son couldn't lead God's church?

Justin Welby's response was breathtaking. He knew that his identity didn't come from who his earthly father was, although I'm sure the discovery was a shock and a hard pill to swallow. He responded by stating that his real identity was not found in his father but in Jesus:

> "I know that I find who I am in Jesus Christ, not in genetics, and my identity in him never changes."[4]

The Archbishop knows that even though our circumstances change, our identity in Christ does not. We may be wealthy business-people one moment and homeless the next, but our circumstances do not change our identity. Identity is not

---

4   "A Personal Statement by the Archbishop of Canterbury Justin Welby", 8 April 2016. Available at: https://www.archbishopofcanterbury.org/speaking-and-writing/articles/personal-statement-archbishop-canterbury (last visited 28 February 2018).

found in who our biological parents are; it is not determined by what we do or who we do it with. Our identity is found firmly in the One who holds us in Himself.

This is the good news. Our adoption into God's kingdom family has moved us into a position where our identity is no longer fixed or determined by outside forces. Our identity is now solidly found in Him. Our identity in God is the only one that can never be changed or challenged by external circumstances: neither relationships nor lack of them, not career choices, bereavement, childlessness, or blessings.

Again... even though our circumstances change, our identity in Christ does not.

Pause.

I want us to pause for a moment and make sure we don't rush on. We could rush past all of this and miss the impact it could have on us. Why not take time to take stock of your life? Can you see any of this in yourself? As I look at the list of orphan behaviours, I'm scared by how many of them I connect with.

If what we know about ourselves governs what we do, can you see how some of your past decisions may have been made out of an orphan complex? Have you felt rejected by others, but now realize that this rejection came more from inside you than from them? Have you clung to something to make yourself feel better, or fought for something that was about you gaining power rather than giving power?

End pause.

GOD IN JESUS RECLOTHES US AS SONS AND DAUGHTERS

If I was preaching now, you would see me getting rather animated. This is where things start to get exciting. This is where God loves us enough to not leave us where we are. I want us to spend some time looking at one of Jesus' most famous stories.

The story of the prodigal son, which can also be called the story of the father with two sons, is found in Luke 15:11–32. In this story we are drawn into a Middle Eastern family conflict. One son wants Dad dead and the other wants Dad's approval. One runs away and one stays at home, hoping that his father will approve of him.

The story unfolds with the younger son running away with his share of the inheritance. Essentially, the boy has divorced himself from his family. He's wished his father dead and orphaned himself physically. The boy doesn't look back but heads into a life of greed, loneliness, and longing. The boy chases after all the wrong things and eventually is left with nothing to call security. We are told that things become so bad he even ends up working for a farmer, like his own father, but this farmer is nothing like his birth father. This farmer owns pigs. Nudge, nudge, this farmer isn't Jewish and has no problem breeding the very animal Jews hate.

The boy is orphaned, alone, and hungry.

Realizing what he has done and thinking his father wouldn't receive him back, the boy decides to head home to try to become a worker on his own family farm. But the story takes a wonderful, grace-filled turn. The original hearers would have been furious or filled with tears because the father sees his son far off and races toward him in a most undignified way, hitching up his clothing, flashing his legs, in a way that Jews would never do.

Then the story gets really good.

The father tells the servants to fetch three things: a robe, a ring, and sandals. Three things are important here. Whenever we see the number three, or see something that happens at 3 p.m., it should always remind us of the resurrection. Remember the story of Peter who denied Christ three times and Jesus three times reinstated him? Jesus practised resurrection on Peter. That's what we are about to see in this story. The father is about to practise resurrection on his orphaned son.

The servants bring out the robe, ring, and sandals. These three items are all significant.

Robes. Remember the story of Joseph and the wonderful coat Jacob his father gave him? Robes were family garments. Some were passed down the family line; others bore the family pattern. Robes became a symbol of the family name. I'm a Rogers. If we didn't have a family name we might have a family crest or even a family weave that we would wear. Robes were symbols of status and family connection.

The orphaned son is presented with a new set of clothes – not the clothes of the farm boy but the garments of the father's family.

Ring. The boy is then presented with a ring on his finger. The family ring was a symbol of family authority. If the father wanted to buy a field or sell some goods, he would either do it himself or send his representative. That person would need to have the father's full authority to do the deal. So a document would have a wax seal to show agreement. The seal would be pressed with the family ring as the deal was legally made.

The son is given a ring for his finger. In other words, his father has given him the family credit card. He is given authority to make deals and trade on the father's behalf.

Remember what Jesus says to the disciples: "Whatever you bind on earth will be bound in heaven" (Matthew 16:19; 18:18). Jesus is saying your deals are the Father's deals.

Sandals. The orphan had returned home with no shoes on his feet: a clear sign that the son was destitute. In the world where the story is being told, the only people who would be barefoot were slaves and servants. So when the father orders sandals for the boy's feet, he is saying for a third and final time that this orphaned son is not to be treated as a servant or a worker but as a son, with all the entitlements attached to that.

The father practises resurrection on the orphan. The boy with nothing, left feeding pigs, barely holding it together, is robed in the family garment, ringed to make legal decisions, and sandalled with dignity, not as a slave.

The orphan is an orphan no more. He's a son, back home, with his father.

You aren't an orphan any more. You're a son or daughter of the most high Father.

You come back to Him and He runs to greet you. His grace is ridiculous toward you. It doesn't matter what you have done; He lifts you up and spins you around. He calls out to His angel servants and tells them to give you the family robe, to place the family ring on your finger, and to put heaven's slippers on your feet.

Drop the mic. Now we are preaching.

Orphan no more.

WE HAVE A PROBLEM... IMPOSTER SYNDROME

If I could end there, I would. But there is a reality we need to face, a reality humankind has created that needs to be challenged. If we start with orphan complex, we end with imposter syndrome.

I get this every time I stand in a room full of church leaders. I look around and start to feel like an imposter. I'm in the room because I am a church leader, but I look at the ability of others and I see their talents and their callings. I look around and start to believe I have nothing to offer because they all appear to be so sorted. So I stand at the edge. I hold back. I believe that they don't need me. I slip out of the door early.

Recognize any of that?

The truth is, we end up feeling like frauds. Sometimes church can be the worst place to be because we look around and think everyone else has it all together, all sorted and worked out. We feel like the one who is faking being a Christian. We say, "If they only knew what I've been doing this week," or, "If they only knew what I've looked at."

We're in the room but we feel unworthy and have nothing to offer. So we slip out early, believing we are worthless.

Remember, what we know governs what we do. If we think we are frauds, then we will behave as frauds.

We have all been told we are sons and daughters, and the Father has put a new family garment on us, He has ringed us, and He has put sandals on our feet. But we end up feeling like we are frauds. The orphan mindset is deeply hidden. We can mask the orphan behaviour, but it still exists. Sadly, this time it's so firmly locked inside us that it's hard to pull out. The roots go deep. But where does this come from?

The truth is, this comes right from the beginning. Remember again the story of Adam and Eve. They have been fathered in God's image and placed in Eden to work with Him and to partner in His plans. But a problem enters Eden. The snake comes along and challenges the heart of Adam and Eve's identity. The snake challenges God's goodness. The snake accuses the Father of lying to Adam and Eve; he tells them that the Father is only after His own gain and that they would be better off going it alone.

This is the one thing that would wreck everything. If the Father isn't good, then neither are we. We are in His image. Adam and Eve are told that the Father they identify with and get their identity from is in fact untrustworthy.

The devil starts the story by telling the kids their Father is a liar, and He still does that today. He tells us:

Your Father is disappointed.

He disapproves of your choices.

He hates what you have become.

The devil says this because he HATES you and will do anything to twist your view of your Father.

We can either be sons and daughters of the devil or sons and daughters of the Father. Which voice do you listen to?

We can say "God loves you" all day long and it won't make a dent, because people know deep down that they don't deserve God's love; it's just too good. But when I'm told that the Father loves Jesus, and that I've been adopted in Jesus by faith in Him, I now have something to put my confidence in, something that isn't contradicted by my knowledge of myself.

Friends, you are loved, not because you're lovely or obedient, but because Jesus Christ is lovely and obedient, and you are in Christ. You have been adopted.

In fact, in our identity as sons and daughters of God, we've been given something far more powerful than an antidote to our failings. We've been given an identity that calls us beyond ourselves and our emotional needs to the story of the glory of God.

Jesus comes to bring us back to this relationship: full adoption into the family inheritance.

STORY OF ADOPTION

A member of my team was talking recently with an amazing young woman in our community. As they spoke, the young woman shared a powerful story of adoption. I only share general details, but still her story is powerful.

This person had been in children's homes, moving from one to the other for many years. One day a woman came into the children's home and picked her out for long-term fostering. The young woman said to my staff member, "I was chosen. That's how I see it." After a year or so of being fostered, she was finally adopted by that mum. The young woman explained, "Being adopted was such a different feeling to being in foster care. Although being fostered was good, because you were safe and being taken care of and had parents, being adopted felt so different, because you knew now that no one could take you away from that family. You were now with that family, not just being taken care of by them, but one of them."

The difference between being an orphan and being adopted is a permanent position of acceptance, love, care, joy, and future. No one can take you away from that family.

Now a slave has no permanent place in the family, but a son [or daughter] belongs to it forever.

John 8:35

God takes away the orphan status to reveal our true identity as sons and daughters. So often we allow our circumstances to create our identity, but in Jesus, as an adopted son or daughter, our position in the family and our heritage do not change, even when the world changes.

SO WHAT DOES THIS MEAN?

YOU HAVE AUTHORITY

Remember the story of the prodigal son? The orphan is robed, ringed, and sandalled. The ring is the family crest for making deals and acquisitions on behalf of the Father. As a family member, you have authority to do the Father's work.

Paul picks up the same idea when he says, "Because you are his sons, God sent the Spirit of his Son into our hearts, the Spirit who calls out 'Abba, Father.' So you are no longer a slave, but God's child; and since you are his child, God has made you also an heir" (Galatians 4:6–7).

This is all to do with inheritance. Remember the girl who was adopted? Before she was adopted, she was living in the children's home with no secure future. There was no inheritance. Then she was fostered. She was looked after, but not given the full position of a family member. She lived with the family but was not a part of the family. But then the day came when she was legally adopted as a full family member. At this point she took on the family name and became a full member of the family, meaning that she now has a share in the family inheritance and is heir to her new father's belongings. With this comes authority to carry the family name, and she is allowed to make legal decisions for the family.

YOU HAVE PURPOSE

You are a *son or daughter of the Most High*, saved from the clutches of the son of the least high: Satan.

With this sonship and daughtership comes a purpose. In your workplace, life, flat, home, street, you are the family priest, pastor, in that place. You are a representative of your family. Wherever you are, you represent the family you are from. This means you represent your Father and you are clothed in the new creation robes of Jesus.

When my twelve-year-old goes to a friend's house, I expect him to behave as I would behave. If he doesn't, it's embarrassing for the whole family. Our purpose is to behave and act as a member of the family and not bring shame on the family name.

YOU HAVE SIGNIFICANCE

Let's pull this all together. Because you have authority as a robed, ringed, and sandalled child of the Father, and because your life now has purpose, you are significant. You are significant because you are a family member, and family members are noticed, loved, and enjoyed. This means we no longer walk with our heads bowed low, but with our heads held high.

Walk with your head held high. Not because you're a champion, but because you're a child of one.

IDENTITY MATTERS

I want to remind us that identity matters, and where you get yours from will make all the difference to your life. In a culture that wishes to challenge identity and leave us confused with regard to who we are, a world where politics is scared to stand up and speak out so appears to allow almost anything to be OK, your identity and what you centre it on matters immensely.

The call of a family member is to live up to and live out the reality of their family identity and to walk with others who are putting on their new selves too.

PRAYER MEDITATION

When you feel that all hope has gone,
  your Father has a fresh word:
"You are My child, whom I dearly love."

When you feel like an imposter,
  your Father has a fresh word:
"You are My child, whom I dearly love."

When you feel you have no future,
your Father has a fresh word:
"You are My child, whom I dearly love."

When the devil whispers that you're an orphan,
your Father has a fresh word:
"You are My child, whom I dearly love."

Amen.

[3]
WE ARE
BEAUTIFULLY
WEIRD

Let's look at where we are up to and where we are going. What we know about ourselves governs what we do with ourselves. Many of us believe and behave as if we are orphans. But this simply isn't true. Jesus has done all He has done, not simply that we might be sinless, but so that we are robed, ringed, and sandalled as a family member. We have a position within this heavenly family.

What I would like to unpack in this next chapter is something connected to your identity, but it is also more than that.

I recently walked into a room filled with women. I was obviously different – especially with my full beard. I didn't fit. The room paused, stopped, and turned. You could hear a pin drop. I apologized and retracted myself from that female space.

As I stepped into that room, something changed. Maybe they sensed the testosterone?

Your presence in a room has an impact. There is something different about the room because you are in it. This is what I want to explore. Many of us believe we don't make an impact and no one notices us. What if there were a shift in the spiritual realm because of your presence? If this were true, how would it change the way you enter a room?

PECULIAR PEOPLE

I have met some odd people, and none more so than in the church. But I get the impression from reading the Gospels that these are the kinds of people God is drawing to Himself. So often we want to fit in, to try to be like others, so we buy the same kinds of clothes, car, and coffee. But maybe God's plan is different from that of the consumeristic society that surrounds us.

The church is made up of misfits, rejects, outcasts – and this is Jesus' body. We don't choose to attend church as a fashion choice; we can't make true Christianity cool.

Peter describes the church as a "chosen people, a royal priesthood, a holy nation, God's special possession, that you may declare the praises of him who called you out of darkness into his wonderful light" (1 Peter 2:9).

The image I've always had of the church is of a group of people who are in the process of becoming more like Jesus. As I read the Gospels, I don't see a Jesus who fits in, but a Jesus who stands apart from the culture and society of the time. Not afraid of it, but different from it – distinctive.

Peter talks about the church as a chosen people, which makes us sound like an elite Christian society. The global church contains many people who behave as though they are God's gift to the world, which I know we are, but they strut around like teenage boys full of testosterone who have just been picked for the football team. Sometimes being known as chosen gives us an over-inflated ego, yet I don't see this in the life or teachings of Jesus. Jesus is confident and passionate but never an egomaniac. The Greek word Peter uses here which has been translated as "chosen" is *eklekton*, which can also be translated as "circled". However, in the King James Version it's rendered "peculiar".

A peculiar people?

The word "peculiar" is often thought of as meaning odd, strange, or weird, but it actually has a much deeper meaning. Something peculiar is something that is irregular, going in an unexpected direction. It can also mean curious.

The King James Bible says that we are a peculiar people, irregular, going in a different direction, and living in a curious way. We're not just set apart; we are also curiously peculiar compared to everything that is often seen as natural and normal.

My translation of 1 Peter 2:9 would read:

> *But you are beautifully weird, colourful in the*
> *grey, a holy tribe, God's treasured possession.*
> *All this so that you may pronounce by the way*
> *you live the praises of Him who called you out of*
> *darkness into His wonderful light.*

Sadly, the church in this generation has become known for being judgmental, unloving, obsessed with what it is against, and hypocritical, none of which were characteristics of Jesus. We are called to be a people going in a different direction, to challenge the systems that control society, and to have a prophetic imagination of a new community in the midst of an old one.

Where is our peculiarity?

Where are we being different?

Where are we making a stand to go in a new direction?

A direction away from Whitehall and the finance district, to go there only to turn over the tables, perhaps.

In 1838, an offshoot of the Wesleyan denomination started calling themselves The Peculiar People. Imagine a church who called themselves The Peculiar People. Imagine how they would have tried to behave and what they wanted to model. They became known for wanting to go in a new, fresh direction, less toward large churches and more toward small, local, grass-roots communities. The movement rebranded itself in the 1950s to the Union of Evangelical Churches and, sadly, it has almost died out today; there are only sixteen communities left. The problem was that people didn't want to be part of a group known for being peculiar. Yet the reality is that the movement was on to something; it had grasped something of Jesus.

There was nothing normal about a Jewish rabbi eating with tax collectors, drinking with prostitutes, and making up His inner group of disciples from terrorists, teenagers, and those with questionable reputations. Jesus didn't come to make bad people good, but to bring dead people to life. To live according to Jesus' teaching, to die to our own needs and greeds, and to have a passion for a life that gives life, means we are peculiar.

The church is a group of people choosing to live out a different ethic, an ethic not focused on self-glory, pride, or building empires, but an ethic that's based on small mustard seeds, little birds, and small children. It's not an ethic of bigger is better, but of smaller and subtler.

Shane Claiborne wonderfully calls the church a "contemporary community of theological pranksters, ghetto poets, guerrilla gardeners and ordinary radicals".[5] There is nothing normal about the church; I guess we can see that by looking around the pews. But what if we were to become known not for our lack of dress sense but for our peculiar passionate love for living justly, searching for creative ways of living peacefully, longing to live with mercy, and walking with humility?

Those who choose to live like this are dismissed as beautifully weird. But then again, so was a first-century Jewish rabbi from Nazareth.

God is different. He is not the same as us. He is not the same as this thing or that thing. Jesus doesn't compare to Gandhi, Buddha, or Mohammed. He is incomparable to anything or anyone else. There is nobody like Him. No other creator. No other saviour. He is unique. He is weird.

5   Shane Claiborne, Christians on the Left conference, 2014.

BEAUTIFULLY WEIRD – HOLY NATION

I want to spend the remainder of this chapter focusing on Peter's phrase that describes God's people as a "holy nation". When many of us think of holiness we have a sense that we are about to be told off for not being holy. Holiness, in our minds, is about doing the right things, doing holy things. However, holiness from a biblical perspective isn't about what we do but who we are.

Sadly, holiness has become about being morally squeaky clean. I want to present us with an alternative way to view holiness. It's a view that isn't determined by you but by Him, something you are not worried about losing, but something you simply *are*.

The traditional view is that Christ died to make us clean and spotless from our sin. We call this "being holy". We link being clean with being holy. This leads us to believe that we have to defend ourselves from the things that will take away our cleanliness.

Some time ago, my son and I were helping to clean out Granny's shed. We went off to the DIY depot and bought these white all-in-one paper suits. You might have seen them: your entire being is protected from whatever task you are about to do. So Isaac and I put on our white all-in-ones and headed into the shed. I noticed Isaac was getting stressed by the spiders' webs and the dust and dirt in the shed. I couldn't see what the problem was. He was in a protective outfit; he was fine. After he jumped out of the shed for a third time, I stopped to ask him what the problem was. He was worried about getting his white suit dirty.

Isaac was more concerned about protecting his white suit than about getting involved in the task.

When we see holiness as defending our white suit, we become anxious about staying away from the dirt. We can't pick up what needs picking up and we can't get up close and personal with the spiders. If the goal is to protect ourselves, then we become over-concerned and defensive, filled with worry, and we come to believe the dirt is more powerful than what we are trying to defend. With this thinking, we conclude that holiness is less powerful than sin.

BEAUTIFUL

The word Peter uses for "holiness" is the Greek word *hágios*. *Hágios* is translated most often as "holy", sometimes as "different" or "unlike", other times as "otherness". The core meaning of *hágios* is "different to and like something". But this makes it sound as though it means "in contrast to something". In the New Testament, *hágios* means "*different* from the world" because it's "*like*" something else: God.

Different to the world and like something else: God.

Holiness isn't simply about avoiding dirt. Rather, it's about carrying God's presence and nature within us.

Holiness isn't about avoiding the dirt; it's a new state of being.

Holiness isn't what we *don't* do but about what we have *taken up*: Jesus, God in us.

Let's go back to the image of Isaac in the white all-in-one. What about if we were to say that holiness isn't about Isaac protecting his white suit but about his white suit changing the environment of the shed? What if the suit was made of something that, when it touched the dirt, neutralized it and then rendered it to a new state: holiness. This new state is wonderful and beautiful. I love to describe this new state as beautifully weird. This is true holiness. It's not something that leaves the world worse off, but better off. It's contagious and looks appealing.

There are two ways of being as Christians toward the world: beautiful or lemon.

There are too many Christians who look more like lemons. They are bitter. Their behaviour is like the behaviour of people who are bitter toward the world. They are judgmental and critical. I want to argue that this isn't what Jesus is like, but beautiful is.

WEIRD

Why weird? Weird means different and strange in the eyes of the world. Jesus looked weird in the eyes of the world because what He did was distinct, different, in contrast in a beautiful way.

My belief is that the Father places His beautifully weird Spirit in us, and this Spirit then makes us more like Him.

Beautifully weird.

This means our engagement in the world becomes about us being a beautifully weird, contagious, life-giving person.

People should say about us, "Wow, they are weird... but boy, are they beautiful!"

With this in mind, let's explore two things. First, where does our holiness come from and secondly what effect does it have on the world? I'll explore it in terms of holiness being something given and something dynamic.

GIVEN

I want to remind us of the story of Jacob and Esau, which is found in Genesis 25. The story goes that Isaac and his wife Rebekah had two sons, one called Esau and one called Jacob. Esau was a hunter-gatherer with ginger hair; Jacob loved to hang back with his mum by the tents. This child had brains, but certainly not brawn, and came out of the womb right behind his brother with his hand grasping Esau's heel. This is why he was named Jacob: the name literally means "he grasped the heel". Esau grew to become a strong, hairy hunter, while Jacob grew up to be the geeky younger brother.

Years passed, and when Isaac was old and had lost his sight (Genesis 27), he called for his favourite son: the firstborn, Esau. Isaac told him to get his bow and go out hunting for some wild boar for him, then to cook it and bring it to him to eat. Isaac wanted to give Esau his blessing before he died.

Hearing all that was said, Rebekah went to Jacob and told him everything. Jacob and his mum planned for him to take the blessing from Esau by dressing as the favoured son. Wearing his brother's best clothes and placing goat fur on his body, Jacob took his father's favourite meal to him. Going into his father's presence, Jacob pretended to be his brother in order to dishonestly claim the family blessing from his dad.

> Jacob said to his father, "I am Esau your firstborn.
> I have done as you told me. Please sit up and
> eat some of my game, so that you may give me
> your blessing."

> *Isaac asked his son, "How did you find it so*
> *quickly, my son?"*
> *"The Lord your God gave me success," he replied.*

Genesis 27:19–20

Isaac evidently had his suspicions, so he asked Jacob to move nearer so he could touch him and check whether he really was Esau. Jacob went up to his father, who touched him, felt his fake hairy hands, and said, "The voice is the voice of Jacob, but the hands are the hands of Esau."

Isaac still wasn't sure, so he checked one last time, asking directly whether Jacob was Esau. Jacob lied and told his father he was.

> *Then Isaac his father said to him, "Come here,*
> *my son, and kiss me."*
> *So he went to him and kissed him. When Isaac*
> *caught the smell of his clothes, he blessed him*
> *and said,*
> *"Ah, the smell of my son*
>   *is like the smell of a field*
>   *that the Lord has blessed.*
> *May God give you heaven's dew*
>   *and earth's richness –*
>   *an abundance of grain and new wine."*

Genesis 27:26–28

The story of Jacob and Esau is one of those stories that is actually about us and Jesus. We see it as a story about two boys, but it's actually a story of humanity and Christ.

Like Esau, Jesus is the favoured son; the son who deserves and is in line for the family inheritance; the favoured son who is in position to receive all the Father has for Him.

Jacob is the least favoured son. He isn't in line for anything. He isn't deserving of the family blessing because he isn't a worthy Jewish man; he is weak and timid. But by clothing himself as the son whom the father loved, Jacob was able to receive his father's blessing. The son who was not worthy of the blessing was able to gain the blessing by placing himself in the position of the favourite son.

Romans 13:14 talks about the same thing: "Clothe yourselves with the Lord Jesus Christ, and do not think about how to gratify the desires of the flesh."

Remember the bit in the story where the least favoured son comes before the father, who says "I hear the voice of Jacob but I feel and smell my son Esau"?

We now stand before the Father, dressed in Jesus' family robes. The Father calls us toward Him. He asks us to speak, then He reaches out to touch and smell us. "I hear the voice of a liar, an adulterer, a fraudster, a thief, a porn addict, and a murderer, but I feel the robes of My Son Jesus and I smell His aroma." And the Father knowingly gives the family blessing. It's important we recognize that the Father *knowingly* gives the blessing. Jacob tricks his father for the blessing, but with us, the Father sees right through what's going on. He knowingly gives us the family blessing. In no way are we deceiving God. In fact, Jesus is pushing us forward and encouraging us. Jesus pushes us forward and steps out of the way.

How amazing is that?

John says it like this: "Even if we feel guilty, God is greater than our feelings, and he knows everything" (1 John 3:20, NLT).

Christ is our substitute on the cross, but Christ is not our substitute in the family of God. We don't trick God to letting us into the family; clothed in Christ, we *are* family. What belonged to Jesus is now given to us because of His generosity and grace.

You might be thinking, "But I shouldn't be here," and you feel like an imposter. Actually, you should be here. You were made for this; this is the location you were always meant to occupy. We can end up thinking we're not really family, that maybe Jesus is embarrassed of us. Jesus is not embarrassed to call us His siblings.

Sister.

Brother.

Remember, Paul writes in Hebrews 2:11 that "those who are made holy ... Jesus is not ashamed to call them brothers and sisters". Jesus is not ashamed, so we should not be ashamed. It's because of shame that we struggle to trust others and we try to provide for ourselves. Some of the most self-sufficient people I know are also the most afraid of being seen as weak.

HOW DO WE DO THIS?

How do we receive God's blessing? To receive the family blessing, all we need to do is stand in the position of Jesus. It's in this position that we receive the blessing; we cannot earn it by our actions. If you want to get wet, you have to get under the shower. If we want to receive sonship or daughtership, we must position ourselves in the flow of it.

What is the blessing? The blessing is about calling down God's hand upon people's lives. When I bless people as a priest, I ask the Father to place His presence on them and in them. This presence is the presence of the Holy Spirit, and where there is God's presence there is power and there is a new reality: a holy reality.

Holiness isn't something earned; it's something that is given. This blessing can only be received when we lay down our old selves and put on our new selves. Jacob could never have received the family blessing if he hadn't got up from his old life and realized that there was much more on offer. Jacob had to actively put down his old self and put on his brother's robes and then go and stand in his father's presence. He couldn't have just stood behind Isaac and reached out for a bit of the blessing when Esau was being blessed – that wouldn't have worked.

Sometimes we receive blessings from our heavenly Father as though they're like those little tasters at the deli counter at the supermarket. We take a little bit and then go back for more if the product's good. But we learn from Jacob that we need to stand directly before our Father and take all the good things God wants to give us.

DYNAMIC

Holiness isn't something static; it's dynamic. It's humming with life, moving, active, and charged. Some talk about *hágios* as meaning something that brings about a positive change in its surroundings. You could say the world is different because of its existence in a clear, positive way, rather like a holy antiseptic.

Remember, the weirdness in us isn't because something is *different about us* from the world, but because we are *like* something else: God, who is holy.

Jesus uses a number of metaphors to describe what we are like. Let's look at a couple of them from the Gospel of Matthew. In Matthew 5:13–16, Jesus describes His followers as salt of the earth and like a city on a hill.

I was in the Judean desert a number of years ago, photographing the landscape for a book I was writing. While I was out there, I was able to visit a small Bedouin camp with a bunch of shepherds. They were sat around a cave, watching their sheep. As I pottered around with my camera, I noticed a large pile of salt behind the cave and decided to ask what it was for. It was the kind of salt you might see in Britain at the side of the road in winter for gritting the roads. But, obviously, a desert in the summer heat has no need of such a thing.

With the help of a translator I was able to get the gist of what the shepherds were saying. They explained to me that when you're in the desert and you need to go to the toilet, you dig a hole, do what you need to do in the hole, and then put salt on top of your waste in order to help it decompose.

The salt acts like an antiseptic. It stops any flies landing on the waste and then on food.

I love the fact that Jesus turns to His disciples and says, "You are salt of the earth." Salt of the earth wasn't used for cooking. This was dirty, gritty salt dug up from the Dead Sea area. It was cheap salt that helped your waste decompose.

I love this picture. It's about proximity. The salt isn't just on top of the waste; it's mixed in with it and helps the waste decompose. The salt makes the waste holy. It's an image of holiness and cleanliness and bringing that into the messiness of life. I love it because that is what we are meant to be: we're meant to be a holy antiseptic in the world, living our lives in proximity to the messiness. Yet very often we do the opposite and separate ourselves from the world.

Your holiness is more potent and powerful than any waste in this world. We don't need to be scared of the world around us, because we bring about active kingdom change, owing to our proximity.

When I was growing up, I was told to stay away from locations that weren't good. I wasn't to go to parties; I was to avoid the "arches" where people read tarot cards. I was also told not to go to a jazz gig because there might be people there doing acid (drugs). I ended up believing that the world was more powerful than the God I followed. I became fearful of anything not associated with Jesus.

Jesus then goes on to describe the disciples like a city on a hill whose lights are shining. The picture Jesus paints is of the city on the hill lit up with many tiny little lights. The lights break through the dark so that the city cannot be hidden.

I love light graffiti. If you haven't ever seen it, give it a Google. People take photographs with slow shutter speeds of people dancing around in the dark with LED torches to create beautiful light images. In these images, the light cuts through the darkness and leaves a beautiful light stain on the image. Darkness hides from the light.

Jesus says the disciples carry something that cuts through the darkness.

Which is more powerful – the darkness or the light?

It's the light, just in case you're not sure of the answer. Darkness is only darkness because the lights have stopped. We can't see light in the light; we only see it in the darkness.

A few weeks ago my wife preached up a storm. She said, "In the day, the small pinpricks of light you make for Jesus look insignificant, but they cause the darkness to tremble."

You are like light graffiti. Your light changes the darkness. Christ's light in you cuts through the darkness and causes it to tremble. There is no need to fear anything of the darkness, nothing demonic or powers of darkness, for we have more power in our little fingers than the dark, because we are Son-lit.

FASCINATION

Some things fascinate us. We can't keep our eyes off them. It might be a view, a painting, a drama, or a person.

Christianity is a peculiar way of living. Christians should be theological pranksters, ghetto poets, guerrilla gardeners, ordinary radicals, and subversive lovers. We should be light in the darkness. We should be pinpricks of light in a dark world that cause the darkness to tremble. Our lives with Christ shining in us should be lived in such a way that we *fascinate* the world.

GATES OF HADES

Jesus had no fear of the darkness. There were regions of Galilee that rabbis would never visit because of the darkness that was associated with them. When the Bible tells us that Jesus travelled to the "other side of the lake" (see, for example, Luke 8:22), that means He went away from the Jewish side to the pagan side. Jesus travelled to areas that were unclean, unworthy, and considered demonic in the Jewish consciousness. We are told that Jesus travelled to the "other side" and cast out demons into pigs.

Another location we are given is found in Matthew 16: the Gates of Hades.

Jesus travelled to a location north of Galilee called Caesarea Philippi. Caesarea Philippi was a deeply pagan

place and would not have been a good place to visit. But
Jesus decided to take a youth group on an outing to do some
sightseeing. Caesarea Philippi was centred on a temple
to a god called Baal. Baal was known as the god of the
underworld and was believed to appear in the springtime. He
was a fertility god and was worshipped at the central temple
known locally as the Gates of Hades. The temple stood tall
against the mountain rock face at the heart of the location.
It was built against a large cave that led down into tunnels. In
the spring, water would swell up from under the ground and
come out of the cave and flow down into the fields. Farmers
would come to worship at the cave, believing that Baal gave
their land fertility. As time went by, a run of steps leading up
to the entrance was built at the temple by the cave mouth.
There, 200 temple prostitutes would dance each day, waiting
for farmers to come and worship Baal, give their offering, and
take them down into the farms and have sex with them to get
Baal's attention.

It's important to note that Baal later became known as
Beelzebub and then Satan. This was Satan's lair where sex
was used as worship. This was the kind of place good Jewish
mothers would tell their sons to keep away from. "You don't
want to go to a place like this – it will taint you." Your white
suit would certainly become unclean. Places like this bred
fear in the Jews.

Jesus took his youth group up to Caesarea Philippi and
stood looking over it. Turning to Peter, Jesus said, "Peter, we
are going to plant a church on this rock and the Gates of
Hades can't stop us."

I was thrilled to visit this location some years ago. What
is noticeable is that there is now neither sight nor sound of
the temple of Baal. It had closed for business by AD 200. And

now there is a church right on top of the rock face. Jesus did indeed plant a church, and Satan's lair could not stop them.

Come on. How great is that?

Jesus didn't feel He needed to avoid the dark places, because He had the light and we today carry this same light.

Jesus walked into a lap-dancing club of the day and planned to plant a church. The activity of the club didn't worry Him, because He knew light is brighter than darkness. That salt is a holy antiseptic.

What is it your Father knows about you?

You are a light in the world, cutting through the darkness.

You are a holy antiseptic in the world, bringing about God's transformation.

(I want to offer a word of caution here. All of what I have said so far and will go on to say is biblical and true. But we also have to be careful. Without wisdom or appropriate support, many things are dangerous. If you are thinking about going to pray over a dark place, obtain wisdom from a church leader, prepare yourself well in prayer, and meditate on Scripture. Jesus' future disciples planted a church at the temple of the Gates of Hell. I am sure they did this supported in prayer and with guidance from those who understood the demonic.)

ROOM CHANGE

As we mentioned earlier, you may not notice, but a room changes when you enter it, because you carry within you God's weird presence. It's a presence that transforms the darkness and renews the filth.

Let's go back to 1 Peter 2:9 for a moment. The King James Version reads, "But ye are a chosen generation, a royal priesthood, an holy nation, a peculiar people."

The Greek here for "peculiar" is the word *eklekton*, meaning "peculiar, irregular, circled, distinct"; something regular doing something irregular. You are strange because your presence is cutting through the spiritual atmosphere and you don't even know it. You look and smell distinct, although you cannot spot it.

And 1 Peter 2:12 goes on to say something quite awesome. I love to translate it like this: "Live such good (beautiful) lives among those who don't believe that, though they accuse you of wrongdoing, they may see your good (beautiful) deeds and be fascinated by them and glorify God on the day He visits us." Live such distinct, beautifully weird lives that you cut through the darkness and present the world with a life of light and antiseptic.

In Exodus 34:29–35 we are told of an incident with Moses. Moses has been up Mount Sinai with God, who has just given him the two tablets of the law. Unbeknown to Moses, his face is shining with a radiant light. As he comes down the mountain, Moses meets with his people, but his face is so bright that they literally have to cover him up. They take a tablecloth and drape it over his face to protect the people from the glory that now covers Moses and shines through him. Once in Sunday school a kid suggested putting a lampshade on Moses. At least that way he could stand in the corner of the room and be useful. Love it – only from the mouths of children.

What does the Lord know about you? He knows that when you spend time with Him your face shines. When we spend time in His presence we are given a glory that shines and makes Him known. I want to encourage us to be less like Moses, covering up the glory, but to be like the lamp that gives light to others, pointing others toward the true Light.

SPITTING IMAGE

When I was growing up, I was frequently told that I was the spitting image of Julian Clary, who was on TV most weeks in the late 1980s. Rather under-impressed with this, I grew a beard so that I would never be told that again. The phrase "spitting image" comes from the "spirit and image". A person who is the spitting image of someone else is the spirit and image of that person. They don't just look like them; they also act like them. Their mannerisms are so similar it's hard to separate them.

We are to be the spitting image of Jesus. We need to be the spirit and image of Jesus. When Jesus walked into a room, everything in the room changed. The rules changed. People changed. Darkness trembled. Jesus entering a place changed it in such a way that resurrection occurred.

What does the Father know that you need to know about yourself?

You carry Jesus. If you have said yes to Him, He is in you. You carry His holiness, and this holiness is dynamic and living. You are holy as He is holy.

Did you know the name "Christian" literally means "little Christ"? You are a little Christ in the world.

PRAYER

Father, I come before You without a long list of things.
I come before You with a desire to seek Your face.
I come before You to seek intimacy with You.
I come before You to encounter Your presence and to enjoy
   Your company.

Reveal what isn't right in me.
Show me what interferes with my time with You.

I come before You without hiding anything.
I come before You to seek Your grace and be caught up in it.

I come before You with the voice of a liar, a cheat, and a thief.
I also come before You with the robes, rings, and sandals of
   Your kingdom.

May I be a holy antiseptic that brings kingdom
   transformation.
May I be a holy light that makes the darkness tremble.

God, may my face shine with Your presence.

Amen.

And the Father replies, "You were born for this."

[4]
WE ARE
POWERFUL

We wake each morning with a battle on our hands. It is a new day and we have to try to make our mark on it. But we struggle, because life is in charge, not us. Things get thrown at us and we feel we are powerless to do anything about them. But this isn't true. Jesus tells us, "You will receive My dynamite" (see Acts 1). We are powerful because His dynamite is within us. The same power that resurrected Christ from the grave is available to us and lives in us, making us more powerful than we can imagine.

Of all the chapters in this book, this may be the one you struggle with the most, unless you're an international reader. We British have a tendency to talk ourselves down. We don't like to appear to be big-headed or "over the top", which means we have strange, fake humility and can be quite self-deprecating.

What we are going to look at in this chapter isn't something that is open to debate; it's a truth about who we are. It's a truth that comes from the mouth of God. He knows this about us, yet we pretend and behave as though it's non-existent. It would be like a battery telling you there was no point you putting it into the TV remote control because it wasn't a battery.

This chapter is about the power God knows is in you and the power that is available to you. It will explain the next piece of the jigsaw of your kingdom identity. You are not an orphan but a holy son or daughter of the most high King. That means there is power from this King that is being bestowed upon you. Exciting stuff!

LET'S START WITH A STORY

This is a story I heard some years ago, told by a Jewish rabbi.

There was once a little boy who was following Elijah the prophet. He saw Elijah doing some great things. People experienced many miraculous signs through this prophet, but these signs left the boy feeling powerless. The prophet was special; the boy wasn't.

Going to his rabbi one day, the boy asked how he could become as powerful as Elijah. He wanted to be special and to have exceptional abilities like the prophet.

The rabbi took the boy to the back of the synagogue and opened the Torah closet, which was filled with copies of the Holy Scriptures. Hidden at the bottom of the closet was a wooden box. The rabbi opened the box and took out an eagle's feather. Handing it to the boy, the rabbi told him that the eagle's feather was anointed and that if he held the feather when he prayed, his prayer would be answered. The boy was overjoyed and put the feather in his leather satchel.

The following day, the boy was walking down the road when he met a sick man in the street. The boy took out the anointed feather and prayed for the man, placing the feather on the man's head. Immediately the man was healed.

The following day, the boy was walking down the street and saw a beggar in the dirt, hand held out. The boy knew he had no coins so he took out the anointed feather and prayed for the beggar, at which point the boy found two small silver coins in his pocket. He handed them to the beggar.

The boy was amazed by the anointing of the feather.

The following day the boy was yet again walking down the street when he came across a woman and a child in need.

They had no food and no means to cook. The boy reached
into his satchel to pull out his anointed feather. He searched
and searched. The feather was gone.

In panic, the boy raced back to his rabbi. "Master, master,
the feather has gone, the feather has gone!" The boy told the
rabbi about the first two men and about the woman and the
child. "I wasn't able to pray, because the feather was gone,"
said the boy.

The rabbi sat the boy down. "My dear son," he said, "the
power was inside you all along because God placed it in you,
not in the feather. Feathers come and go, but the power in
you is beyond your understanding. YHVH sees what you are,
not what you are not. He sees what we are and what we can
become. The power is given to you; the feather was just the
tool for you to find it."

There is more to you than meets the eye. Held within you is
treasure you have yet to discover. It's a treasure your Father
has already given you. The prayer is that we get to see it, use
it, and be like Jesus.

THE TWO F-WORDS AND THEN THE OTHER TWO F-WORDS

There are lots of F-words in this next section. However, these
are not swear words.

There are two F-words that dominate us and hang over and
under our lives. These F-words define much of who we are and
the hopes we have for the future.

James 4:14 says that our lives are like "a mist that
appears for a little while and vanishes". Our life is but a

fleeting moment. Perhaps because of this we try to control it, to do as we wish, and claim authority over it. But there comes a time when we realize we aren't really in control. Things are out of our hands. We make mistakes. Things fall apart. We become sick. We become tired.

Over our past we see written the word FAILURE. Our past is riddled with failed opportunities, failed examples, failed relationships, failed finances, failed applications, failed marriages, failed hopes and dreams. For so many of us, failure is the bright banner over our lives.

This then governs how we see our future. So there is a second F-word: FEAR. Because of our past failures, we look forward with the eyes of failure and we see nothing but fear for what could be. We believe that our future will just be like the past. We have seen how the events of our life have panned out, and we believe things will continue in the same vein.

So our past is defined by our failures and our future is defined by our fears.

I want to be really honest for a moment. I find it's really easy to trust God with my eternal future. There is nothing I can do that will make my eternal future more secure. It's all in the hands of Jesus. But when it comes to my earthly future, I find it harder to trust in the same way.

I trust God with my eternal life, but I struggle to trust Him with my credit card bill.

I trust God with my eternal life, but I struggle to trust Him with my children's education.

I trust God with my eternal life, but I struggle to trust Him with my retirement.

We can feel powerless over our future. We can also feel powerless because others take power from us. They can force us to bow to their pressure. They can force us to play their games. Landlords have power over us when they say, "Pay me more or move out." People force us to go at their speed. Someone else's negativity or disillusionment means we feel trapped and powerless. Not only do we take our own power, but others take what remains.

What about you? Are you the same?

My future is tinted with fear. What if I don't have job security? What if we don't own a house when we retire? What if my kids make the wrong choices? What if I can't afford to repay the debt?

With these two F-words, we look and act powerless in many situations. Because of this we struggle with the idea of being powerful. We allow our circumstances to dictate how powerful we feel, and often they make us feel powerless. Rent, debt, the supermarket queue: they all leave us feeling as though things are out of our hands.

Let's look at the example of the disciples for a moment. Jesus had died and the disciples had run away. They were hiding in the upper room in fear of the Jews and the Roman Empire (John 20:19). The disciples allowed their earthly view of their circumstances to dictate their view of their power and position. Jesus had died, so they had failed. Because they had failed, they hid in fear of their lives.

We look at our own failures.

We feel powerless with regard to our sin and actions.

We feel powerless when we have been sinned against.

We feel powerless in various situations – traffic jam, work, court, supermarket queue.

Our own attempts to feel that we are in control make us feel even more powerless.

Our own ill health or that of a loved one and the inability to do anything about it makes us feel powerless.

Our power does not start with us or our circumstances. Our circumstances change, but He doesn't. Our power does not start with us; it starts with Him.

The reality, friends, is that our lives are broken into two halves: the past and the future. The beauty of God is that He holds our lives in His hands like a long length of string. In the presence of God, the past and the future of our lives are merged, like a tangled cord, into one.

In Jesus, we are presented with two better F-words over our past and future. Because of Jesus, the whole of our past is brought together into the word FORGIVENESS. The whole of the future is in the safekeeping of the FAITHFULNESS of God.

Our past is found in FORGIVENESS, not failure.

Our future is found in His FAITHFULNESS, not fear.

It's in this place, between these two F-words, that we find ourselves. In this sobering place we are reminded that we are broken but forgiven; that we aren't the Saviour, but He is. It's in this place that we see, sense, and experience His faithfulness for the future.

Dietrich Bonhoeffer writes:

> We never simply live the present, for both the events of the past and the expectations of the future influence it. The good things of the past sustain us in the present and the hope of the things that are yet before us confidently draw us into the future. At the same time, we need to receive healing from those things in the past that were less than good by extending forgiveness to those who have hurt us; and we need to trust God for his FAITHFUL PARTICIPATION in the things that are yet to come.[6]

So our past is behind us, held in the firm grip of forgiveness, and our future is found in God's faithful participation.

Because of this we can breathe deeply. We aren't the Saviour; we don't need to be strong like He is. The good news is that He is on our side: the side of our past and the side of our future.

This is about His capabilities and His love for us, not our capabilities and our love for Him.

WHERE DO WE START?

A question we have ask is: where do we start when it comes to power? Do we start with ourselves and our limitations, or with Him and His power? Starting with ourselves will always get us the same results: failure. Too often when looking at a problem we start by looking out our own resources to solve the problem and we become overwhelmed, and we never get to a place where we can look at His resources.

ACTS 1

The book of Acts is essentially a book about the activity of the Holy Spirit working in and through God's people. As we read the stories we start to see that where the presence of God is, there comes with it the power of God. The Person of the Trinity known as the Holy Spirit is the presence and activity of God in the world. He is the power of God active in and through the lives of people as well as being active as a Person Himself. The book of Acts allows us to see how people change

6   Dietrich Bonhoeffer, *A Year with Dietrich Bonhoeffer: Daily Meditations from His Letters, Writings, and Sermons* (Zondervan, 2006) (capitalization mine).

when they encounter this powerful presence in their lives. Those scared teenage boys and girls became courageous and active children of God. Their fear was met with the power of God, and their fear was transformed into courage.

The book of Acts starts with the disciples gathering with Jesus moments before His ascension. The disciples asked Jesus what they presumed the whole resurrection was about: "Are you going to restore the kingdom to Israel?" The disciples had a narrow view of what Jesus' activity, life, death, and resurrection were all about. Jesus is offering mankind something much bigger than the restoration of the nation of Israel: the restoration and empowering of all things, all peoples, and all nations.

Turning to them, Jesus announced, "I am going to fill you with power to fulfil the Father's plan. You will be My witnesses in the religious places and the non-religious places."

Jesus told them to wait for His gift. God's power is a gift. The question for the disciples was: were they going to run and HIDE in fear or run and WAIT in faith? I wonder if your position sometimes is hiding from God rather than waiting for God.

CONTROL

The disciples asked Jesus whether He was going to give control back to the Jews. This was a key question for the Jews, who felt their world was out of control. They wanted to know that Jesus was going to give them the upper hand, but Jesus moved past their desire and offered them what they really needed: kingdom power.

Why would Jesus want to give us power rather than control? The disciples were imprisoned by the desire for

control. As we read the Gospels we find the disciples
desperate to understand and control what was going on.
Judas tried to control the events by handing Jesus over to the
Jews. Peter tried to control by offering to build Jesus a tent to
house Him and the prophets at the transfiguration. James and
John tried to control who would sit on Jesus' right and left. All
the disciples in the boat during the storm woke Jesus up to
stop it. Control was a problem for the disciples – and I would
argue it is for us too.

Control is ultimately about reliance. Who do you rely upon?
Is it your knowledge that makes you feel secure? I recently
spoke at a gathering, and immediately after I had finished
speaking someone in the room came over to tell me I'd got
something wrong. Their desire to be in control gave them a
need to come and tell me the moment I'd finished so they
could feel more powerful, or more in control than I. I always
appreciate feedback, so I received it with grace.

Jesus wants us to know less and rely upon Him more. He
wants us to have continued reliance. This taps into one of
the problems we have in the church: we want to work out the
future, but He wants to work in us for the present.

Jesus wants to challenge us to give up control, which,
if you remember, is at the heart of the orphan mentality.
Trusting someone else is a problem for us when we believe
only we understand and only we can be trusted. Trust and
control are key issues Jesus wants to challenge as He moves
us to trust Him. If as orphans we only trust ourselves, it
becomes easier to control what's in front of us rather than
allow ourselves to trust Him.

The unprotected heart feels safer if we seek to control our
world through knowledge. The irony is that true safety comes
when we trust our heavenly Father. This is exactly what we see

in Eden: the snake tries to give knowledge over trusting the Father. The disciples want to know what's happening. Jesus tells them to wait for power.

LET'S TALK ABOUT POWER FOR A MOMENT

Through life we promote our power in a variety of ways. In the 1980s people talked about the "power suit". Now we do it through the brands we wear and the clothing we choose. In the workplace the suit may be powerful, but in the fashion industry a particular elite designer might carry more power. We also feel that we gain power through how many Twitter followers we have, or subscribers on YouTube. Such power can be rather niche. My son watches a YouTuber who has millions of followers. But no adult has ever heard of him. We think power comes from who you know and what you know; others would say it's how much you give away knowledge that makes you powerful.

Either way, all this communicates that we think power comes from what we possess. But this isn't power; it's influence. It's what we use to influence the environment.

The power that we are going to talk about is very different. We are going to explore how it's the Spirit of God that makes us powerful.

Jesus tells His disciples that they are going to "receive power when the Holy Spirit comes on you". What is this power He is talking about? The Greek word in this passage is *dunamis*, from which we get the word "dynamite". Jesus is saying that when the Holy Spirit is active in your life, you receive power that's like dynamite.

Many churches look as if they need a bit of rocket fuel inside them. But this power isn't a power that is expected.

When a rocket is lit and the rocket fuel is on fire, it creates a controlled explosion and things start to move. This *dunamis* is a power that is almost unexpected; it's miraculous and supernatural. This dynamite is God's power, and it's surprising to all who receive it.

This is a power that is manifest not in supernatural moments but in natural and normal moments. Think about the queue at the supermarket, the school playground, the bus stop. It's in the natural and the normal that this supernatural dynamite is revealed. The Spirit seems to be more active on the high street than in the church. It's where He is least expected that we see Him the most active. Remember Peter and John going up to the Temple? They were walking up a set of steps when they were stopped by a lame man. It was while they were doing something they did most days that they saw the dynamite of God most powerfully at work.

When you receive the Holy Spirit, it's as if you have dynamite: dynamite in your prayers, dynamite to get things done, and dynamite in your words. The disciples proved this to be true. These ill-educated fishermen became the most powerful preachers and teachers the Gospels after Jesus had seen. The Holy Spirit unlocked something within the disciples and they became like dynamite.

But why did they need to become like dynamite? This outpouring was about the disciples having what they needed to thrive, receiving all that God had for them. And the consequences of this were that everything was different: their confidence, who they believed themselves to be. They saw the truth of their sin and the good news of the cross. Everything started to make sense.

This outpouring of the Spirit has a purpose. It's not simply about people thriving; it's about going further with the good news we carry. Remember that Jesus said, "You will receive dynamite and you will be My witnesses in the religious places and the non-religious places." The work of the Holy Spirit pushed the church further than it had been before, and the same is true with us.

I wonder how many of us carry this powerful dynamite but struggle to acknowledge it and access it. Maybe we look at ourselves and see vessels that don't look that special, and we write ourselves off as unvalued.

JARS OF CLAY

Paul knew exactly how we might feel. Why would God put something so powerful into vessels that simply look unworthy of their contents?

During the time of Paul, homes were difficult to protect. It would have been difficult to hide valuable items. Doors didn't have substantial locks on them, and windows were open with no glass. Homes were at risk to intruders, so valuables were therefore vulnerable. To get around this, people would hide their valuable things in clay bowls, jars, and bottles. They would put the valuable item at the bottom of a jar and then fill it with rice or maize. That way a burglar wouldn't know what was in the jar. Putting your valuables in clay pots was the best way of looking after your treasure.

Paul writes in 2 Corinthians 4:7–12:

> But we have this treasure in jars of clay to
> show that this all-surpassing power [amazing
> dynamite] is from God and not from us. We are
> hard pressed on every side, but not crushed;

perplexed, but not in despair; persecuted, but
not abandoned; struck down, but not destroyed.
We always carry around in our body the death
of Jesus, so that the life [resurrection] of Jesus
may also be revealed in our body. For we who
are alive are always being given over to death for
Jesus' sake, so that his life may also be revealed
in our mortal body. So then, death is at work in
us, but life is at work in you.

God is placing His treasure in us for safekeeping. He's putting
His treasure in us because He thinks it's the best place to
keep it, and in doing so He shows that it's not something
from us but something from Him. We are cracked pots,
broken and chipped, weak and delicate. We look at the jar of
clay, yet Jesus looks at the treasure. His dynamite lives in us,
like treasure.

I don't want to rush on before we look at one other point
from this passage in Paul's letter to the Corinthians. Paul
writes that we are perplexed, persecuted, and struck down but
not in despair, abandoned, or destroyed. I want to speak for a
moment into the lives of those who feel perplexed and struck
down. Some of us live constantly in a state of depression,
anxiety, and worry. Some of us worry a little; others are
anxious a lot. We can end up feeling we are struck down, on
our knees, unable to get up. I want to say something about
God's power in this.

It's at those times when we feel the most powerless that
God's power is the most powerful.

We are not talking about our own power. When we hit
difficult times, whether it's the winter blues or a wall of
depression, we in ourselves have little power. The winter can

seem as though it will never end, and we can't see the light. But the truth is, He is powerful, and He is powerful in us.

I have a beautiful friend who has struggled with depression for many years. He loves Jesus and longs to be completely free from his depression. We were chatting recently when he said this:

> Some mornings I simply can't get out of bed. But then I remember that Jesus has given me all I need. I don't feel it or see it, but I trust it is true. So I force myself to get up. I force myself to get dressed, and I force myself to leave the house. But I still don't feel His power and ability. Sometimes it's not until the end of the day when I look back I see He has in fact been there. Even though the depression means I don't see and the anxiety is like a tight collar around my neck and ears, I realize I did get out of bed and I did get dressed and I did leave the house and I did make it through.

His divine power gives us everything we need – through His glory and goodness. My point is this: some of us, when we talk about being powerful, struggle to imagine a scenario where we might feel able to even get out of bed, let alone do anything supernatural. Don't allow the anxiety and depression to tell you that you aren't able, because with Him all things become possible.

Allow Him who made you and saved you to tell you what's possible, not the lies we are told by the illness.

SOME OF US HAVE A BIG "BUT"

Even with all that has been said, many of us still have a big "but". We say, "But you don't know me. I can't. It's not going to happen." We are full of the buts. The problem here is that we are still living as if we are in control.

Being in control will only ever leave us tired, worried, and stressed.

Stop trying to control everything and allow the One who is fully in control to take over.

What is it our Father knows about us? We are cracked, we are broken, we are vulnerable. This means we aren't able without Him, but with Him we are. He knows that with Him we are powerful, because He is powerful. Any excuses are because we aren't trusting Him; we are trusting ourselves.

If we believe we are weak, we will behave as though we are weak. But when we know our Father is powerful, we will enjoy His power.

We may know that we are powerless and say yes to God's power, but it is possible still to live as if we are in control. It's possible for God to be handing us His power while we stand there with our hands closed, claiming we aren't powerful, and remaining in control. To receive His power we have to allow ourselves to drop everything and be open-handed.

DROP THE NETS

Let's think about Peter for a moment. Peter was approached by Jesus. Peter stood on the beach, holding his fishing nets, and Jesus called to him, "Peter, follow Me" (see Matthew 4:19). For Peter to follow Jesus and to step into all Jesus had for him, he had to drop the nets. He had to hand over the keys to his fishing boat and he had to follow. To follow Jesus is an active thing. If we aren't moving forward, we will ultimately move backward. Unless we let go of the nets and open ourselves up for new things to be placed into our hands, we can't follow.

Imagine Peter trying to follow Jesus with fishing nets firmly in his hands. "I'll follow You, Jesus, but I'm dragging my business with me."

What do Peter's nets represent? They represent our view of ourselves, our ego, our vision for our lives. It might be our business, like Peter; it might be some other form of security. So often we want Jesus' power but we don't want to free up any space for it.

I remember when I was a child my mum would say to me at the beginning of December, "You need to clear some space for your Christmas gifts." But I didn't want to get rid of anything. I wanted to hold on to everything. Sometimes our hands are full of the wrong things, so we struggle to receive the good new things.

On holiday this summer, my son had been collecting stones and his pockets were full. He then saw a beautiful piece of wood. But his pockets were full, and the weight of the stones was pulling his trousers down. We told him to pick up the beautiful piece of driftwood, but he couldn't because he was holding up his jeans.

Peter was called to follow. To follow meant dropping the things that were holding him back, slowing him down, pinning him to the beach. For Peter, to follow meant to walk with Rabbi Jesus and accompany Him in His work. To follow Jesus meant to get involved in the signs and wonders that Jesus was doing. Jesus knew when He called Peter what Peter was going to be capable of. Not because Peter was capable, but because he was available and the powerful God could use him.

Paul writes in Romans 8:11 that "the Spirit of him who raised Jesus from the dead is living in you". The same power that was in Christ was in Peter and Jesus' other followers, and now the same power is living in us. Our problem is that we look at our human hands and we see human fingers, and we don't think we can change or do anything. But God doesn't look at our hands; He looks at what He is placing into our hands. We don't look at our past, because He doesn't: He looks at heaven's future, and so should we.

EPHESIANS

There is a wonderful passage in the book of Ephesians where Paul writes a prayer for the church in Ephesus. During this prayer, Paul writes about God and who He is and what He is capable of:

> *Now to him who is able to do immeasurably*
> *more than all we ask or imagine, according*
> *to his power that is at work within us, to him*
> *be glory in the church and in Christ Jesus*
> *throughout all generations, for ever and ever!*
> *Amen.*

Ephesians 3:20–21

One of my issues is that I allow my past to dictate my future. I look at what I've been able to do before and then I assume that's the limit for everything going forward. I have a tendency to cap God and His power.

Do you ever feel as though you are at the end of your energy; not only physically but also emotionally and spiritually? Some of us have been running this race for so long that we are dangerously dehydrated.

What God knows about us is that He is calling all of us into a *radically empowered life* that we could never achieve in our own strength. Jesus tells His church that there is immeasurably more on offer than just a religious life, a good life, or a moral life. There is more to offer our families and friends, more to offer our neighbourhoods. God knows that He is offering us an immeasurably more powerful and beautiful life, but He also knows we allow ourselves to be governed by our past.

To a dehydrated, unimaginative, paralyzed church, Jesus announces that MORE is always on offer.

God has more for us to *receive*,

more for us to *become*,

and *further* for us to go.

Jesus wants to empower us by His Spirit.

The word "empower" is a fascinating one. We can often think of it as a physical power, but in fact it means to be authorized, inspired, and enabled. Jesus wants His church to be authorized to do the works of His kingdom, inspired to dream bigger dreams, and enabled to do the work, not under our own strength and power but His.

So where do we go from here? How do we leave the land of no imagination for an adventure across the open seas, caught up with all that God has to offer us? The point is this: we can try to build our confidence, work on our self-loathing, but these things will fall into place when we receive an appropriate vision of our Father. When we come to the place where we see Him as the all-important One and we are able to drop our nets and follow, then the other things will all fall into place. When He becomes our glorious vision, everything else falls away.

Tozer puts it beautifully: "The heaviest obligation lying upon the Christian Church today is to purify and elevate her concept of God."[7] In other words, the biggest task we have today as Christians is to sort out our view of God. We have shrunk Him down; we have boxed and contained our vision of Him. God needs taking out of our religious buildings, out of our manmade boxes, so He can expand and fill our vision once more.

There is a wonderful story of Elijah that comes from the mystic tradition of the Jewish faith, and was told to me by a Jewish mentor some years ago.

The story goes that one day Elijah is walking down the road when he notices a man carrying a box. The two men greet each other and Elijah recognizes him as the local idol collector. The idol collector and Elijah get talking and the man asks to show Elijah the box he is carrying. The box is made from beautiful olive wood with gold trimmings. Inside his box are a number of stone and marble idols. The man even boasts that he's drilled a hole in the box to let the light in so the idols can see.

The idol collector asks Elijah whether he has a box for his idols.

Elijah cheekily but beautifully responds, "The One I worship made the box. So no matter how much we ask, He refuses to get in it."

I love Jewish humour.

Nothing has changed. We still create boxes to try to contain God and His power. These boxes might not be made from olive wood and ornately painted with gold leaf, but we do create them in our hearts.

---

7   A. W. Tozer, *Knowledge of the Holy* (Authentic Media, 2005), p. 4.

We have imagination boxes that say God only answers some prayers.

We have imagination boxes that say God only loves good people.

We have imagination boxes that say God doesn't heal.

We have imagination boxes that say God is smaller and much less powerful than He really is.

We have imagination boxes that say God lives in religion.

We have imagination boxes that say God only loves Christians or is only available to Christians.

As Elijah said in the story, my God made the box and He refuses to get in it. No matter how big the box, it will always be too small for an Immeasurably More God. Until we can allow our imaginations to fill with God, we are going to struggle to imagine that we are powerful through Him.

PRAYER MOMENT

Take a moment to offer your imagination to God. Confess your lack of imagination and invite a God imagination. Ask Him not just to fill you with power but also to reprogram your view of yourself: a cracked pot filled with treasure. Ask Him to reveal this to you.

THE ROOKIES

I want to tell you a quick story about power. When I was twenty-one I was playing in the university squash league. If I recall correctly, I was in the semi-final and playing against the college number two. Andy was a good player, and I knew

I needed to put everything into my game. Late in the game Andy hit the ball by the right wall. I dived and hit the wall with a thump. Immediately I felt pain along my arm. We carried on playing, and I went home in agony after losing the game.

Two weeks went past, during which time I noticed a lump on my shoulder which caused me constant pain. I ended up going to Accident and Emergency on a Friday afternoon. They X-rayed my shoulder and it turned out I had broken my shoulder blade and probably had a trapped nerve too. The bones were on top of each other and I would need an operation to sort it out. The lump on my shoulder was the size and shape of an egg, so I'd named it my "egg". They sent me home with a sling and told me to return the following Monday to see a specialist.

That Sunday night I went to a church that wasn't my usual church. I sat at the back with my arm in the sling. The pastor stood up at the end and announced that God wanted to heal two people that night. One of the people had an "egg" on their shoulder.

How awesome is that?! I didn't know the leadership and they didn't know me, but God had told them my secret name for the lump on my shoulder.

I refused to go forward, believing God could heal me right where I was. After the third announcement about the egg, I found myself going to the front, where I was introduced to their prayer team. I was gutted: I found myself presented with a prayer team who were around fifteen years old. They told me it was their first night and had only been shown what to do that afternoon.

Great. I'd been given the rookies.

They prayed for me, and I stood there with little faith.

But as they prayed, my shoulder became warm. I started

to notice it was becoming wet with sweat. As they continued to pray, the pain left, but I could still feel the egg on my shoulder. I thanked them and went home, rejoicing that God had at least stopped the pain.

The following day I visited the hospital, where they X-rayed me again. The doctor stood in front of me with the two X-rays side by side. Grunting, he left the room, saying they must have X-rayed the wrong shoulder. Five minutes later he returned, saying it was the correct shoulder. I told him how I had been prayed for the day before and the pain had stopped. The X-ray showed that the break had gone: although the egg was still there, the shoulder had healed over the weekend. I said, "Wow, it's a miracle!"

His response was more cynical: "Some people heal quicker than others."

Some people heal quicker than others... Healed in four days? I don't think so.

My point is this: I got the rookies. I got the kids who had only been shown what to do that afternoon. I got the ones who had never seen a miracle before. But God is the powerful one, not the rookies.

You might feel like a rookie. You might feel you have little to offer, that you have no abilities. But let me tell you this: God loves the rookies, because the rookies know they aren't able. They know they need God to show up so that things will work out OK.

Rookies aren't able, but they are available.

What is it that God knows about you? He knows that He has dynamite for you, should you be willing to drop the nets and follow. Peter dropped the nets and followed. He followed until he found himself in an upper room, where he waited, and then everything changed.

PRAYER

As we finish this chapter on power, I want you to read this
blessing over yourself. It's a blessing that sends you out from
the pages of this book with power into the world and into your
life lived each day in the "normal" places.

Go in the power of the Holy Spirit,
to build the kingdom that is here and now,
and wait faithfully for the kingdom that is yet to come.

Father, send us out with Your powerful Spirit,
to live and work to Your praise and glory.

Amen.

[5]
WE ARE ABLE
AND CAPABLE

We try to negotiate with God. "God, when I have learnt more, been to Bible class, got more experience, THEN I will do what You want me to do, but I'm just not able to right now." This way of thinking is toxic for us. The idea that we need more "something" stops us from being everything we are capable of being. We aren't able because we are clever, beautiful, and strong, but because He is able through us. "His divine power has given us everything we need for a godly life" (2 Peter 1:3).

In this chapter, I want to explore ability and capability. We are able, not because we have been trained up, or because we know more than others, but we are already able because of Him. One of the things that frustrate me is the idea that we have to go to Bible school to become empowered in the Jesus movement. I learnt a lot at Bible school, but I have learnt more by getting on with what God asks me to do in situations right in front of me. Planting a small church in the middle of a skate park wasn't a result of any cunning plan or because I was ready, but because God had a plan and I was there at the right time to join in with what He was doing.

In this chapter we will see that God uses those who are in the B Team to do the A Team work.

WHAT HE SEES

We were at the coast and I was teaching my son to ride the waves. The waves were beautiful. Each wave was coming in at a regular pace and was clean – perfect for riding on the board. Every time Isaac went out, a wave would hit him and he would run back and tell me he couldn't do it. The truth was, I knew that if he would just push off before a wave, the wave would catch him and he would ride it to the beach. To ride the wave wasn't in his ability, but the power of the wave would carry him.

Isaac eventually came to me and said he couldn't ride the wave. I looked him in the eye and said, "Isaac, I know you can ride the wave, but you won't be able to do it if you're scared of the wave. The wave is nothing to be scared of. Trust me: I know you can do it."

Isaac went out and caught the next wave – and it was a big one for his height.

Sometimes our ability only needs to be our availability, because the wave will do the hard work. It has the power; we just need the availability.

Isaac couldn't see how he could ride the wave, but I could see what he was capable of. I knew my son, and I knew what he could become.

We see what we are not; God sees what we are and what we can become.

There is more to you than meets the eye. This isn't hype; it's the truth. There is more to you than you believe you are capable of. God made you and watches you and knows you better than you know yourself.

The Message translation of Romans 8:27–29 says this:

> *He knows us far better than we know ourselves, knows our pregnant condition, and keeps us present before God. That's why we can be so sure that every detail in our lives of love for God is worked into something good. God knew what he was doing from the very beginning.*

GOD KNOWS YOU BETTER THAN YOU KNOW YOURSELF

You may think to yourself, "I've already tried that before, and I don't see my ability." The truth is that God knows you better than you know yourself. God knows you are able and capable and you will be OK. You are capable when you rest in God's strength and not your own.

> *You know when I sit and when I rise;*
> *you perceive my thoughts from afar.*
> *You discern my going out and my lying down;*
> *you are familiar with all my ways.*
> *Before a word is on my tongue*
> *you, Lord, know it completely.*

Psalm 139:2–4

As I read Psalm 139, I am reminded just how intimately God knows me, and it makes me stop and think. Do I even know what I am going to say before I say it? It seems that God knows. He knows each and every one of us on planet Earth better than we know ourselves. Matthew 10:30 reminds me that God knows even the number of hairs on my head. But it doesn't just stop there: God knows me beyond the physical facts of my body. He knows more about me than my height and blood group, even more than the doctors know.

God knows every one of my thoughts, my motives, my hopes, and my dreams. For many of us, this might feel frightening, but stop and pause for a moment. God doesn't know these things so He can catch us out, but He knows these things because He cares about and loves us.

God knows what you are capable of, the dreams you could dream, and how you have abilities beyond your imagination.

When a farmer plants a young apple tree, he knows what the tree is capable of producing. So he plants the tree in a space that it can grow into. God knows what you are capable of and He has planted you in the culture and community you are in so that you are capable of bearing much fruit.

Peter writes in 2 Peter 1:3–4:

> His divine power [dunamis – power, strength,
> and authority] has given us everything we need
> for a godly life [eusebeia – devout practices
> or functions relating to a supernatural persons
> and powers; a life that reflects God] through our
> knowledge of him who called us by his own glory
> and goodness. Through these he has given us
> his very great and precious promises, so that
> through them you may participate in the divine
> nature, having escaped the corruption in the
> world caused by evil desires.

I would like to translate Peter like this: "We have escaped death so God is giving us access to His divine life so we can do what He does *with* Him." In other words, "God knows you are able, because He knows He is able."

THE DEN

We recently built a den in the garden. It's pretty awesome. We have slept out in it a number of times now and it's such a beautiful place. The den stands off the ground on stilts, with a 10 foot by 8 foot base. It's big! My son Isaac wanted to build a den, so I worked with him to make it a reality. I bought the bits, climbed into skips to get wood, and found the nails and screws we needed. Isaac still believes today he built the den – and he did, pretty much. But I was with him during the whole build, holding and supporting. I did the bits he struggled to do, but he did most of the screwing with the electric drill. He's eleven and quite proficient with a power drill and sander.

If I had left Isaac on his own to build the den, I'm not sure what we would have ended up with. But I knew what we could do together, and I was able to work out the plans and then work with him to build it.

I knew what Isaac was capable of because I knew what I was capable of.

THIS IS NOT ABOUT GIFTS AND TALENTS

You might have noticed that the next chapter is about gifts. I purposely placed this chapter before the next one. So often we believe our ability is dependent on our gifting. But this is about us being able, before we talk about gifting. We are talking about being able because of Him and what He knows about us.

Your ability to navigate life, to walk as a follower of Jesus, and to be involved in His activity in the world isn't dependent on your gifting. Your ability is determined by what God states to be true in the very core of who you are. Imagine there are two layers to your being: the inner nature and the outer nature. This isn't entirely correct, but work with me for a moment. Your gifting is your outer nature, what is placed upon you. And then there is the inner nature: God knows you are able because of who you are in your inner nature. You are created in the image of the Creator. This means your ability is found in this core place of your being. You then have giftings placed upon you, but this is on top of your ability.

If it were about your gifting, then working on your gifting would be the sole route to doing something, or to doing it better. But before your gifting is imparted, there is simply you, and God knows the simple you is enough.

You are enough.

Why?

Because "we are God's handiwork, created in Christ Jesus to do good works, which God prepared in advance for us to do" (Ephesians 2:10).

You are enough, because the One who worked on you says so.

WE ARE ENOUGH BUT WE DON'T BELIEVE IT

We can be told constantly we are enough and that we are able, but we have this underlying belief that we simply aren't. It's like an underlying guilt that lurks around the dark edges. For others of us, it's not even lurking: this belief that we aren't able or enough affects each layer of our lives. We end up believing that we are poor parents, poor partners, poor work colleagues. We feel we are constantly letting people down, and this belief becomes loud and insistent in our lives. For some of us, this has been a lifelong problem, a clear but faint voice that whispers, "You can't, you aren't able, you aren't enough. You let yourself and others down."

There can be a number of reasons we feel like this:
Habit.
The voices of others.
The voice of the deceiver himself.

HABIT

We all have bad habits. Some of us bite our nails; others bite their lips; some eat to punish themselves; others habitually drink too much. There can be a fine line between habit and self-harm. The truth is that habits become self-harm when they are not good for us. A habit is a settled or regular bent or practice, especially one that is hard to give up, that is affecting us. We can have positive habits, such as reading Scripture, prayer and worship, and daily practices that lead us to the mirror that reflects our true identity.

We can also have toxic habits that tell us things that are simply not true about ourselves. Because of this, we have to be proactive in keeping our habits in check. We must exercise the practice of regularly looking at our internal and external habits.

Our internal habits most likely come from an internal voice that tells us certain things. We need to be able to see this voice for what it is and refuse to believe everything it says. This toxic internal voice grows like a weed. It starts with a little seed planted in us and then grows until it affects the whole of us.

We must turn away from the habit of listening to the internal voice and turn to the habit of listening to the Holy Spirit, who is the only voice that will speak truth.

There is a massive difference in these two voices. The voice within us will condemn, but the Holy Spirit comes to convict. When the Holy Spirit convicts us, He speaks specifically about sin and not about who we are. He loves us and wants to help us work on our sin. To get to the place where we do not listen to the voice that tells us, "You're not enough," we have to turn up the voice that says, "You are enough." If we allow Him to, God will drown out the toxic voice.

THE VOICES OF OTHERS

The internal voice can sometimes be planted by others. A little snide comment, a flash of a raised eyebrow, or an unhelpful comment can plant a seed in us that grows and takes over. We can be left feeling insecure by a comment that we perhaps don't understand grows to affect our whole confidence. I find that with most people I speak to on issues of lack of confidence, behind all the internal voices is a comment or a hurtful view from someone that has grown and developed and become something of its own. What are the voices you have heard spoken over you?

There is a wonderful story in the Gospels about a woman who had been bleeding for twelve years (Matthew 9:20–22; Mark 5:25–34; Luke 8:43–48). She would have been pushed out from her village because of Levitical laws around uncleanliness and monthly bleeding. People would have thought she was bleeding because of judgment upon her from God. "She must have done something wrong; she must have slept around," people would have said. Children may have called her names: "There is the bleeder."

Here was a woman who was out of the village, which means she would have been pushed out of her family, and consequently out of God's blessing. One day she heard Jesus was in the city, so she covered herself up and went looking for

Him. She had heard that this rabbi had healing in His hands. There was a Jewish idea that the Messiah would come with healing in the wings of His garments. If only she could touch Him, she might be healed.

The woman found Jesus, reached out for Him and touched His clothing. Instantly, she was healed, and instantly Jesus realized something had happened. He turned to the woman, they spoke, and He blessed her before she left.

What was her identity?

Orphaned.

Outcast.

Bleeder.

Unwanted.

Unclean.

Jesus turned to her and said, "Go in *shalom* [peace], Daughter."

Daughter. In that one moment, Jesus gives her a new identity. She now has an identity not as village outcast but as a member of the family. She is adopted. She has been listening to the voices of those speaking curses over her, and Jesus comes and speaks a fresh word.

What are the voices you are hearing? What do they say?

Jesus leans toward you right now and looks you right in the eye. "Son, Daughter."

Jesus says you are enough. He says you're a son or a daughter. Hear what He says. Let His voice cut through the hustle and bustle of the crowd. Let all the toxic voices fade away as He speaks new names over you.

THE VOICE OF THE DECEIVER

The name of Satan in the Hebrew Bible is *Asatan*, which literally means "the deceiver". The devil comes to deceive each of us. He works tirelessly to undermine and condemn. He strives to separate us out and cause tension between us, and plants seeds that grow into destructive plants. Our minds become gardens full of weeds that tell us we are a mess, unable, and unusable. Because of the weeds that are growing because of *Asatan*'s seeds, our gut reaction to things will be to say no, and be defeated.

This conviction from the enemy comes in subtle but wide-ranging ways. He aims to condemn you and make you a defeatist. He wants you to feel defeated before you even try. Trying might give you hope, so he knocks you down before you try. He wants to constantly lead you back to your own abilities. He wants to lead you to the place of trying harder next time, to a place of having to stay a learner. If only you knew more, you might have more confidence. He wants to keep you trapped in the place of making a plan of action and dreaming up ideas. Like addicts, we can vow to change ourselves as much as we like, but we will only end up back at the place where we started. We will always end up back in a place riddled with guilt, feeling condemned and that we aren't enough.

When we are in this place, we can try all the self-help books in the world; we can aim to build up our self-esteem, listen to people's positive praise, and gain superficial confidence, but the reality is that these are nothing more than crutches. The reason the devil's words are so powerful is that they are true, and he knows it. He knows that we aren't enough, so he plays on this. The only way of dealing with the power this has over us is to do the one thing we think we shouldn't.

We would say the devil is a liar and we shouldn't listen to him but, in fact, sometimes what he says is true. We need to agree with him to break the power of his words. We need to agree with his words and then add to them. This may feel counter-intuitive as we fight this battle: surely we don't let the enemy win over us? Trust me: this is a powerful move that will lead us to a better, joy-filled place.

We have to say, "I am not good enough, BUT God is."

"I'm not good enough, BUT Jesus is."

Rather than continuing to go back to the place of self-effort, we must come to the place of adding those three words: "but Jesus is".

At this point, your left hook leaves the devil powerless. He has no follow-up move, and no way of undermining the power of this. Jesus is enough. So you are enough.

As Peter puts it, "His divine power has given us everything we need" (2 Peter 1:3). The key word here is "everything" we need. You see, it starts with Him and ends with Him, His glory, and His goodness.

We can contradict the voice of doubts with the voice of truth:
I can do all things through him who gives me strength.

Philippians 4:13

"My power is made perfect in weakness."

2 Corinthians 12:9

HE IS ABLE – THEREFORE WE ARE ABLE

A. W. Tozer writes, "How completely satisfying it is to turn from our limitations to a God who has none."[8]

You are limited, but in Him you find a new "you". When we turn from our own limitations we find a God who is limitless. Tozer says this is "completely satisfying". We can rest, knowing that He is able and therefore so are we.

We don't need to be able to hold it all together all the time, because God holds it all together. We just need to be satisfied that He is the limitless God, and in His limitlessness all is well.

We are able because He is able, because His power, strength, and ability are made known in our weakness.

It's in our weakness that we find He is all we need. When we are trying to hold it together, we can't see how He might be needed. We are holding it, so why should He? But when we hit the place of weakness, we find the satisfaction that all is well in Him.

In this place of satisfaction the deceiver will come and whisper lies. He will whisper, "You can't do it," but our response becomes, "Nope, but my God can."

Ezekiel says in 43:2 that God's "voice was like the roar of rushing waters, and the land was radiant with his glory". God's voice is louder than the sound of rushing waters. Do we allow space to hear this roar of the waters? Do we allow the hope of Jesus to breathe into our lives, or do we limit ourselves? Which voice is dominant? Can you spend time listening to a better voice? A stronger voice? A more liberating voice?

---

8   A. W. Tozer, *Gems from Tozer: Selections from the Writings of Tozer* (Wingspread Publishing, 1980), p. 3.

Sometimes we get stuck; we can't do anything. We look at ourselves and feel paralyzed. We feel unable and powerless. Sometimes we just need to move a little to see how He is good, to position ourselves to listen to the roar of the waterfall.

You being able and enough is not about you; it's about Him. It's about God's constant love and God being able.

All the time, He is able, and therefore so are we.

Paul understood this when he wrote, "For when I am weak, then I am strong" (2 Corinthians 12:10). The problem is that we get this muddled. Our greatest strength is in fact our weakness, and God is strong in us at our weakest point.

TICKETS AND INVITATIONS

I want to end this section by talking about tickets and invitations. There is a fundamental difference between a ticket and an invitation.

With a ticket, you pay for it and then you have to prove you have it. If you lose the ticket, that's tough. A ticket is something you have received because of a transaction. You need to keep it safe or it will lose its power. A ticket is like a key: if you don't have it, you can't get in.

But then there are invitations. Invitations are given from people who want you to attend their event. Invitations come from friends who know us, from people who want us there. Invitations are received with the joy of the giver. With an invitation, even if you lose it, you are still invited.

We are invited into the divine nature. God is inviting you into Him. You don't need to keep a ticket polished and clean. You have an invitation card, but you don't even need to have it with you because the invitation is open; your name is written on the list.

So what if we knew that God knows us?
God knows us, and He always did.
You are known by God; you aren't just another human. You aren't just another name. You have significance and worth because you are known by Him.

One of the biggest insecurities in millennials is fear of insignificance. It drives us to want attention from others. To be known and to feel significant is one of the biggest drivers within the millennial generation. This is why so many people want to be on *The X Factor* or one of the other Saturday night talent shows. Our world is permeated by a "celebrity culture". People want to be known, not for doing anything specifically, but for existing. The YouTube culture is telling young people that value is found in how many viewers you have on your channel. This is why some people behave like "God's gift" to the world: it's the desire to be significant. For the millennial generation it's not about what we can do. It's not even about being good at anything. It's about being known, receiving the most views, subscribers, or "friends".

When it sinks in deep that our Father knows us, then we don't need to live in the light of other people's opinions. When we know we are known, we live in His acceptance. Without this identity we try to carve out a place for ourselves to be seen, yet He has already given us a name: Son, Daughter.

Sadly, we can believe that our best self is tied up in the praise that comes from other people, but this is simply not true. This is where consumerism kicks in. If we aren't known, if someone hasn't spotted us and celebrated us, then we need to find something else to fulfil us. So we get stuff in an attempt to be happy with who we are. We consume in order to be enough, without realizing that we already are enough.

QUESTION

Do you behave as though you have a ticket, or an invitation? Do you know that you are known by God, or do you behave as though you have a ticket to keep polished?

To conclude, what is it that He knows about you? He knows there is more to you than meets the eye. He knows that you are able and enough. He knows that you can navigate whatever is ahead because He is able and He is clothing you and residing in you. He knows that you are invited into His divine nature and are able to play your part in it.

TO DO

You are invited. Your name is on the list, and I have personally invited you. You don't need to keep this invitation. It just exists.

[6]
WE ARE
GIFTED

Let's do a quick recap. Over the chapters of this book we have been thinking about what it is that God knows about us. These are things that we may have thought about before and forgotten, or perhaps for the first time our eyes are being opened to our position, value, worth, and ability. The trouble is that we look at others and look at ourselves and feel inferior. We all do this. We believe others are having a great time and doing well while we sit there and feel lonely, insecure, and worthless. There is a word for this: FOMO.

FOMO is the Fear Of Missing Out.

Social media has perpetuated this feeling of FOMO. We look at others and think their social media page is full of activity and friendship; we see what they do and how they are living their lives, and we feel we can't compete.

In this book we have been seeing that our identity is firmly tied in to our Creator. We are adopted as sons and daughters; we are given power and holiness, which all creates the environment for us to be able because He is able.

I now want to move us on to the next step of thinking about gifting, and the devil's work of comparison. In Romans 12, Paul writes to the church about the gifts bestowed upon them by God the Holy Spirit:

We have different gifts, according to the grace [God's generosity] given to each of us. If your gift is prophesying, then prophesy in accordance with your faith; if it is serving, then serve; if it is teaching, then teach; if it is to encourage, then give encouragement; if it is giving, then give generously; if it is to lead, do it diligently; if it is to show mercy, do it cheerfully.

Romans 12:6–8

There are more gifts than the short list we see here. We can look at some of those later. But what interests me are the "different gifts ... given to each of us". In other words, God has a gift bank, and His gift bank is full of wonderful things, and all people are given some of these things. It isn't that the religious elite get the best gifts and everyone else gets the leftovers. It's not that only some people receive gifting and the rest of us sit back to see what they can do. Each of us has gifts; the question is, will we use them and build them up?

Gifts are like muscles. We have to exercise them and become proficient in using them.

I was at a conference recently where I found myself giving a talk on the gift of creativity. If you ask a roomful of people to raise their hands if they think they are creative, most people will not budge. The truth is, we can all draw in some shape or form, but many of us haven't given time for the gift to develop. During the lunch break, a group of attendees made it rather clear to me that they were mathematicians and scientists and simply weren't creative. I pulled out some index cards and gave them out, along with standard black pens. Placing a mug in the centre, I invited each of them to slowly look at the mug, to see its shape and how it looked in the space, and then to try to do a line drawing of it. There were two distinct groups that emerged: those who gave it a go and those who wouldn't even entertain the idea.

Those who gave it a go did really well. Many of us think a drawing needs to look like the item. That's not necessarily true: think about impressionist art. The purpose of creativity isn't to make a replica of something but to enjoy the process of making something.

When we announce, "I'm just not a creative person," we are really saying we have given up on the idea of trying something and pressing through. I recently got back into drawing. My first drawings were quite bad – my daughter's eyes looked so wonky she was unrecognizable – but I pressed on. The drawings over the following weeks were somewhat OK, and then something clicked and I'm enjoying drawing again.

The difference between someone without a gift and someone with a gift is the willingness to give something a go. It doesn't necessarily mean you will be the world's most gifted person, but it's the stepping out that allows you to investigate. It's in the risk-taking that we are able to explore and investigate what is a natural gift, a developed gift, or a given gift. Just because we try, it doesn't automatically make us gifted in a new area, but the risk-taking gives us the opportunity to grow and develop.

TWO TYPES OF GIFTING

I want us to think about two areas of gifting: natural gifting and supernatural gifting. The reality is that I don't think they are separate. I firmly believe a gifting is a gifting and all the gifts are natural and supernatural at the same time. However, for the purposes of this book, I want to pull them apart for a moment.

Each of us has "natural" giftings. Some of us talk about having a creative gift or a management gift. Some of us are leaders and others are supporters. Some are gifted in sport and others in DIY. Some of us will recognize a gifting in the area of hospitality, caring, or loyalty. Yes, loyalty is a gift some of us possess. Some of these gifts we learn at school, in the workplace, or at home. There is a chance we look down on some of these gifts and see them as useless.

Sometimes when I'm talking with people, they will say they aren't gifted like others are. What they mean is they don't think they have what they consider to be the "special" giftings that others have.

We see ourselves as "normal" and others as "special". These "special" gifts, as some people think of them, are gifts of prophecy, teaching, healing, tongues. You get the idea. We can end up behaving as though these gifts are exceptional and more important than other gifts.

I want to make something clear: I do not in any way believe that the gift of DIY is in any way a lesser gift than the gift of prophecy. Both are about seeing what is possible in the midst of chaos. When we behave as if some gifting is more important or exceptional, then we tell people there is a hierarchy – that some people are more important because their gifts are more important.

But the truth is that all gifts come from the heart and character of God. Prophecy, accounting, healing, cleaning, administration, tongues, preaching, and hospitality: all are natural and supernatural, and all gifts are available to all people.

Now, obviously all of our brains work differently. We see things differently and we have talents that stand out over other talents. But what has intoxicated the church for many years is a view that some people are special and others aren't.

I want to unpack this in three areas: the little we have in our hands, the problem with the gifted and talented, and Dad has a toolbox.

LITTLE IN OUR HANDS

We can look at the little we have in our hands and we can
see little, or we can see treasure. My son caries around in
his pockets what many people would see as junk. I asked
him recently to empty his pockets: he had a conker, string, a
penknife, a paper clip, and some other bits and bobs.

Isaac's pockets are full of junk. But what I consider to be
junk is in fact Isaac's treasure. Isaac loves creating, and he
even runs his own YouTube channel on crafts. Isaac can often
be found with a roll of tape, some string, and some clips, and
he's making some wonderful thing. Last year he found a bike
wheel in the graveyard. With the help of some yogurt pots,
paper, paint, and tape, he turned it into a three-foot wide
spacecraft. Isaac has a track record of using the bits and
bobs in his pockets to make something cool.

Isaac uses the little in his hands and it becomes
something amazing. He doesn't see junk; he sees opportunity.

What's the difference between what's in Isaac's pocket
and what's in my pocket? It's attitude. Do we choose to see
potential or do we choose to see limitation? Some of us would
say that we are realists, but maybe being a realist means we
don't see a new reality.

God has a track record of doing great things through less-
than-great people.

B TEAM

I want to come back to the B Team for a moment. The
disciples were high-school dropouts, terrorists, and thieves.
But Jesus saw the little they were, knew their potential, and

called it out of them. Jesus wasn't looking for gifting or talent; Jesus was looking for willing hearts. Would they be willing to pick up the pen and paper and give something new a go?

The B Team were the people who were willing to be used; they dropped everything and followed. I'm a little curious as to whether Jesus approached anyone who said no. Was it that the disciples were the first and only twelve, or did Jesus walk the beach the day before and get turned down a few times? Just a thought.

The disciples had little in their hands. Peter owned a fishing fleet and he and his friends worked as fishermen. Some of the disciples were known members of terror organizations, and others thieves. They didn't have a great list of credentials. Their pockets were almost empty. Yet they had passion, and they carried the desire to learn.

One day, Jesus had been teaching and the disciples were sitting listening to him, along with thousands of others. The Rabbi turned to them and announced that the people were hungry and needed feeding. The disciples were left for a moment to come up with a solution to the problem. The problem was that their hands were empty; they didn't have many options. They found a small boy with a packed lunch and they brought him to Jesus, but it just wasn't going to be enough.

The point of the feeding of the 5,000 story is that it wasn't important how many loaves and fish the boy had. The point is that it wasn't enough. And yet, for God, our scraps are enough. Jesus took the scraps and they fed 5,000 men, in addition to the women and children (John 6:1–13).

We make the story about what Jesus did, which I would agree is a major plot point, but we often miss the main point. Human beings have little in their hands. Whatever we could come up with would never be enough. It's only through Jesus and His power that our little becomes a kingdom amount.

What are the scraps in your pocket?

We see our little and disregard it, while Jesus sees our little and He asks us to offer it.

WHAT HAPPENED TO THE PICCOLO?

Sir Michael Costa, the great nineteenth-century conductor, was one day in an important rehearsal for an evening where a huge choir would join them for a major event. The orchestra and the choir were all in the room with the conductor, practising and making a lot of noise. At the side was a piccolo player. The piccolo isn't a loud instrument; in fact, it is often seen as a minor instrument in the orchestra.

As the rehearsal went on, the piccolo player was enjoying the choir so much that he chose to stop and listen for a moment. Soon after he did so, Sir Michael stopped the whole rehearsal and questioned, "What's happened to the piccolo?"

The Great Conductor notices and needs us to complete His orchestral masterpiece. We think we will not be noticed but He notices, because the little has a major effect on the whole.

The Conductor notices when you don't use your little for Him, when you keep your little in your pocket. He knows when something doesn't sound right.

THE PROBLEM WITH THE GIFTED AND TALENTED

When I was at high school they had just started to develop a programme for the gifted children. They now call it the

"Gifted and Talented". They would take the top 10 per cent of the year group and give them extracurricular help, an extra push, because they were very able. The problem for me was that I was nowhere near the gifted and talented. I was more ordinary and plain. I would sit at school and see others picked for the sports team, others picked for the main parts in dramas, and others picked for the gifted and talented pool. As I sat there and looked at those who were chosen, I started to wonder: if they are the 10 per cent, then what does that say about the 90 per cent? In other words, the 90 per cent must be the normal, the plain, and the untalented.

If there is a gifted and talented pool made up of the top 10 per cent, what does that say about the 90 per cent?

The issue is that comparison is the killer of gifting. If we look at the 10 per cent and see the gifted and talented, then we must be the "other" group. We sit back and judge ourselves against everyone else and write ourselves off.

I wasn't among the gifted and talented; I was in the no-hopers pool. I struggled, unaware that I was dyslexic, and found school more than frustrating. I could never see how school applied to life. We never seemed to do anything that used my set of talents in a way that would give me direction and hope. Things were so rough that when it came to my exam results, I went to collect them wearing a T-shirt that simply read "LOSER". For me at that time, it was the truth: I was a part of the bottom 10 per cent, not the top.

I wonder where you would see yourself. Would you be among the gifted and talented? Would you be among the no-hopers, or somewhere in the "normal" middle? It can be very toxic to see ourselves as middle-ground people. We can see ourselves as one of the crowd, with little to offer.

BARRIERS

There are two barriers that can stop up from seeing ourselves
as the Father sees us. These two barriers leave us thinking that
we have little to offer and that there is little gifting within us.
We either compare ourselves with the wrong people or we live
with the fear of failure. These two barriers stop us from seeing
the potential or the gifting that we hold. Both of these barriers
are the work of the deceiver, who seeks to undermine the truth
about us.

I want to spend a moment looking at these two barriers to
see where they might be affecting our own self-view.

WRONG COMPARISON

Theodore Roosevelt once said "Comparison is the thief of
joy." I would agree with him: as we compare ourselves with
others we will always be left stripped of our joy – either
stripped of the joy of appreciating ourselves or because
we are mentally attacking someone else. Not only do we
compromise joy, but we also compromise any sense of beauty
in ourselves. We end up looking at the treasure someone else
has without seeing the diamond we have.

I heard a story many years ago. I'm not sure if it is true
or not; it was told to me as if it was, but no search on the
internet has enabled me to find it.

The story went that there was a Russian farmer who had
many fields full of cattle and sheep. He wasn't wealthy, but
neither was he poor. He became aware that on the farm
next door the farmer had found a source of gold on his
land, but the farmer was not interested in the money, as

he was growing old. One day the first farmer read the local newspaper and discovered that the second farmer had died and his land was going up for auction. He decided he would sell his own land and buy the old farmer's land, and maybe he would find more gold. So he sold his own land and bought the farm and mined the gold. He made a tidy sum from the purchase and was pleased with what he had found.

A couple of years passed and the farmer was reading the local newspaper again. It turned out that the new owner of his old land had found oil. The oil was worth millions and the new owner was set to become a very wealthy man.

Sometimes we can look at what others have and be green-eyed, wanting what they have, and we miss the wealth we have right under our noses. We can see what seems to be easy wealth for someone else and miss what we might have with a little work.

We can see ourselves as a brick of coal, but beneath the black dusty surface there could be a diamond.

If you were to look at a painting by one of the masters you would probably say, "I could never do that," and in reality you probably couldn't. Only a small number of people could produce a master painting... that's why they are called masters. We compare ourselves with someone who has exceptional talent and then wonder why our self-esteem is low. Too often our self-confidence is built upon comparison with others; we think we can't do what they do, so we don't do anything. We think we aren't as talented or gifted as they are, so we imprison ourselves in a room called "comparison".

We say, "I can't."

So we don't.

And therefore our value in ourselves decreases.

Dr Kristin Neff, a leader in the field of self-compassion research, explains:

> The pursuit of high self-esteem has become a virtual religion, but research indicates this has serious downsides. Our culture has become so competitive we need to feel special and above average to just feel okay about ourselves (being called "average" is an insult). Most people, therefore, feel compelled to create what psychologists call a "self-enhancement bias" – puffing ourselves up and putting others down so that we can feel superior in comparison. However, this constant need to feel better than our fellow human beings leads to a sense of isolation and separation.[9]

I don't know what you think about that quote. Dr Neff says that comparison will leave us isolated and separated. I believe this is true. I believe this is a clear and divisive work of the deceiver himself. If he can leave us feeling inferior, or if he can leave us destroying others to make ourselves feel better, we will end up isolated, lonely, and imprisoned by our own imagination.

I will be honest with you: I do this, and I believe we all do it, on some level. We compare ourselves with others to help mask our own feelings of self-disappointment. We human beings have become competitive in order to impress, or we have relinquished our own needs because we have devalued ourselves through disappointment. This behaviour will always steal our joy and leave us feeling lonely and worthless.

9   Dr Kristin Neff, "Why self-compassion is healthier than self-esteem". Available at: http://self-compassion.org/why-self-compassion-is-healthier-than-self-esteem/ (last visited 5 March 2018).

So what are we doing when we compare ourselves?

My wife is a big *Doctor Who* fan. In the *Doctor Who* TV series, when one doctor dies he regenerates into another doctor. It's a cunning way of having multiple actors play the same character, as one actor retires from the part and another comes in. What I have noticed is that people will always judge the new actor based on their first episode and the last actor on their last episode.

Comparison is always unfair. We compare the worst of ourselves with the best we presume about someone else. Our comparison is never equal. We overlook the bad things others do and only see the good, while taking into consideration our own worst behaviours or gifts. Our way of measuring isn't real comparison.

Comparison will rob you of being who you are meant to be. Comparison makes no sense when we realize that our gifts, talents, abilities, successes, and contributions are unique to each of us and our purpose in the world. We can't compare ourselves to others, because their role and mission is different.

We have more to lose in comparing ourselves to others than we have to gain, as we essentially hand over our pride, dignity, drive, and passions to someone else. If I were to judge my baking against my wife's, for example, I would never bake and I would leave my enjoyment at the door. Doing this always leaves the focus on someone else. I can only take control of my own life; I can only enjoy what I partake in myself.

We had a baking event at our church recently and a number of people didn't take part because they knew that two or three prize bakers would be entering the event, so they didn't even try. They knew they weren't going to measure up in comparison to some other people, so they didn't join in, and they were robbed of the enjoyment they could have had by being involved. Comparison will never give us value, a sense of fulfilment, or meaning. It will always leave us resenting others and ourselves: "Why can't I do something like them?"

We control our activity of comparison, not the master painter or the prize baker. When we compare ourselves, we will always be left in a negative space, and the effects are far-reaching.

FEAR OF FAILURE

The other barrier we face is fear of failure. Because of this fear, we fail to explore what it would mean to even give something a go. We don't want egg on our face, so we don't have a go at making the omelette. Fear of failure makes us risk-averse. If we don't risk anything, we believe we will not be disappointed.

I have never heard anyone get to the end of their life and say, "I took too many risks," although I have heard people say, "I wish I had taken more risks." People get to the end of their lives and take stock, and many come to realize that by playing it safe they missed out on adventures. They stayed close to home to be safe, and then realized there was much to see that they never saw.

Some of us might have an ingrained fear of failure, and this fear might come from our schooling or our parents. It is plausible that one generation's fear of failure becomes the next generation's narrative. I have known many young people who aren't given the confidence to do something because their parents are fearful in their own lives. They then hand this fear on to their children as a way of making themselves feel secure.

The reality is that risk-taking and failure aren't bad; the only failure is to never fail. Failing becomes another way to learn. Risk-taking and getting things wrong becomes a gift to each of us. It is something else we now know doesn't work, which means we are on a journey of figuring out what does.

The truth is, we aren't fearful of failure; we are fearful of ourselves. We have linked failure with our self-identity, self-esteem, and self-confidence. We think failure says something about us personally. "I must be a failure myself, because only failures fail." Wrong. If we see life through this lens, we will be paralyzed by fear.

If this is our mindset we will think:

If I fail, I AM a failure.

If I lose a game, I AM a failure.

If they turn me down, I AM a failure.

If I lose my joy, I AM a failure.

If my Facebook post doesn't get more than ten likes, I AM a failure.

No one texted me today; I AM a failure.

If I don't get the loan, I AM a failure.

If you think this way, you will always place yourself in the failure bin. But the truth is, any risk-taking is a win. Putting yourself out there is a win. You become successful because you dared to fail.

So where does this fear of failure come from? I have a theory. This way of thinking comes from the way we do school. At school you take a test, you are ranked, and then you are placed into classes dependent upon your ability. There tends to be a link between behaviour and ability. The children who behave are the ones who listen, and therefore they do better academically. The children who come low in tests see themselves as at the bottom of the pile. The reality is that on such a scale there will only ever be one person at the top and the other 99 per cent will be behind. Fear comes because we think we are our test results. I didn't do well, so I'm in the lower quarter and therefore my value is low. We think our test results are a reflection of ourselves.

This way of thinking is paralyzing and creates a lack of separation between who we think we are and the results we get. We then take all this thinking about comparison and fear and place it upon our relationship with God. It affects the way we expect God to bless us, and we become mentally second-rate Christians.

BACK TO THE PASSAGE

Let's go back to the passage for a moment. Paul writes in Romans 12:5–7:

> In Christ we, though many, form one body, and
> each member belongs to all the others. We have
> different gifts, according to the grace given
> to each of us. If your gift is prophesying, then
> prophesy in accordance with your faith; if it is
> serving, then serve; if it is teaching, then teach.

This passage tells us a number of things:

1. "We" are ALL gifted. Stop looking at what others have and start to see what you have. We are all gifted, so stop looking at the gold in the other person's hands and see the oil that you have.

2. "If your gift is ..." Our gifts are varied and not all the same. We each have different gifts. If we keep comparing, we will all want to be preachers, worship leaders, and prophets. God has gifts for you that fit your specific passions and joy, characteristics and abilities.

3. Availability. It's about willingness, not success. Gifts aren't determined by your ability, but by your availability. In Romans 12:3, Paul writes, "Do not think of yourself more highly than you ought, but rather think of yourself with sober judgment." In other words, be honest about who you are. Are you available for the gifts God has for you rather than looking for the gifts that aren't for you right now?

4. "In Christ". Your value is not found in your gifts but in your "family identity". It's "in Christ" that we find our proper place, not in the club where all those with particular gifts gather together.

DAD HAS A TOOLBOX

My dad had a toolbox. In fact, he had many toolboxes, drawers, and cupboards, and so did my granddad. We would watch *The A-Team* on television on a Saturday evening and then we would head out to the shed to build something out of the scraps of wood and metal around the shed. I used their tools – they were made available to me. I became proficient in using power tools because I knew I could get them out and use them whenever I wanted. My use of them wasn't limited.

God has a toolbox, and we are invited to use the tools it contains. God's kingdom tools are available to us to use whenever we want, and the use of them isn't limited. The only thing that will stop us from taking them out is the fear of failure and wrong comparison. We will think that we can't try them out until we have learnt how not to fail, but failure is one of the best ways to learn.

What's in your hands? What are your strengths?

MAKE A LIST

I want to invite you to write a list of your gifts, talents, and abilities: everything from the silly things to the great things. You could write, "I make a good cup of tea," or, "I'm OK with numbers," to, "I can preach at missions and everyone will come to faith."

Once you have made your list, take a look at it. Which do you consider to be useful gifts and which aren't? Then I want you to ask another question: who says so? You? God? Sometimes God has great plans for our "silly little gifts". The fragments of part gifts can look like nothing to us, but they look like great treasure to God.

Take a moment to pray, inviting God to grow and expand your gifts. Ask Him to do away with your fears and wrong comparisons. Ask Him to reveal to you your identity as a treasured son or daughter who is encouraged to use the family toolbox.

PRAYER

God, breathe life into me; make more of what I have.

God, breathe life back into the image of You in me; dispel my self-rejection.

God, remind me that I am made in Your creative image; reveal to me my creativity.

God, show me Your toolbox; place tools in my hands. I want to be available.

God, push me forward to rummage around the family toolbox and try new things.

Father, I have fear. Please help me.

Father, I compare myself. Please clear my mind.

Show me what You see.

Thank You for knowing me better than I know myself.

Amen.

[7]
WE ARE
AUTHORIZED

We are CHILDREN of God,
SERVANTS to one another,
But RULERS against the enemy.

We sit back, waiting for permission to live our lives. We wait, as if someone needs to give us permission to start living and acting out what's deep in our hearts. If we are waiting for someone else to give us permission to start doing what we should be doing, we will be waiting for a long time. We need to realize that Jesus authorized us in His death and resurrection to do the work we have to do, and at Pentecost He commissioned us with His Spirit. So what are we waiting for?

We are full of good reasons to wait a while, aren't we? It's too hard. I'll wait until it gets easier. I'm too old to get started now; the youth have the energy and ideas. What will other people think? People will not accept me. This isn't the best time; things are all up in the air. The pain of stepping out isn't worth it. I've not been given permission.

Let's remind ourselves what we have learnt so far. God has taken off the orphan to reveal our true identity. We are our Father's children.

But what does this mean?

It means that He has robed, ringed, and sandalled us. He has given us a new identity as a holy antiseptic that is powerful and gifted. The very nature of your new self is as someone who has authority because of who you are, not because it has been given to you.

Why does bleach have a cleaning and sterilizing ability? It's not because it's been given to it; rather, it's because, at the chemical level, that's what it is. And the same is true with us. We are authorized to do what has been ordained for us, not because the church tells us so but because the Father has changed who we are and positioned us with this new "composition" that in its very nature is authority.

THE PAUPER OR THE PRINCE

Do you remember the story of the prince and the pauper?
If not, it's worth a read or a watch. I want to draw out the
identity of the two characters of the story. The story revolves
around two characters: one is a pauper from birth and the
other is a prince. In the story, they swap places, and we see
how each of them engages with his new world.

Let's take a moment to consider what it means to be
a pauper. The word "pauper" is Latin and translates as
"poor". It engages with the financial poverty and also with
the mentality of the poor person. Nowadays we talk about a
mentality that goes alongside someone who is poor. This isn't
always the case.

I'm generalizing, but there are some helpful things to
think about when it comes to poverty. Poverty is more than
not having money; poverty is about all areas of our lives. The
poor have levels of poverty in their lives that stop them from
moving forward. The pauper mentality is something we can
carry with us every day. We can walk around believing that we
are victims of the world and of the behaviour of others. This
can leave us with the mentality that we are in our nature a
victim of others.

Obviously, there are circumstances where we truly are
victims. I don't want in any way to undermine the injustice
of a crime done to us. I'm talking here about those moments
when we have a "poor old me" view of our lives. The pauper
mentality is when we consistently regard ourselves as victims
of the negative actions of others. We presume that others
have the power to change things while we don't. We blame our
misfortune on someone else's misdeeds. We believe we are
powerless, and we believe this is just how things are.

I was chatting recently with a woman who shared her story with me. She came from a broken family, and from a young age had always believed that others had a better deal than she did. She ended up falling into drugs and drink, believing that it was everyone else's fault for not stopping her. She believed that others needed to take care of her and that she was powerless to make a stand against taking drugs. She ended up with a long list of debts because she spent everything she had on heroin. The phone company cut off her landline and the electricity board cut off her power. She believed at this point that they were being unfair, even though she was thousands of pounds in debt. The housing association sent her an eviction notice because of the months of unpaid rent. She stormed into their office, claiming they were being harsh, even though she had ignored all previous bills and letters. Claiming they had forced her into a corner, she tried to burgle a property to get money, but she was caught. When she sat in the police station she told the officers, "It's the housing association's fault."

This lady's life had been ruled by the mentality that others should solve her problems, others should pay out, and others should carry her. One day, sat in a recovery meeting, she came to a realization. She was behaving as if everyone else had authority over her life and that she was a victim. She realized that the only victim she was, was to herself. She had led herself down the path to where she now was. She told me she realized she had to take some responsibility for her actions.

Years down the line she is now a Christian. She came to realize that her core identity was broken, and she had been playing out a daily narrative that she had made for herself.

She came to realize that in Jesus she was not a victim but something far more.

But let's not look at someone else's story and see the pauper mentality in them. Let's look at ourselves:

Where do you believe you are a victim?

Do you play out a narrative where you think others are in charge of your life?

Where do you behave as though others have control?

Have you blamed your misfortune on someone else's deeds?

Is there an area of your life where you need to take responsibility?

It's easy to skip by those questions because they are hard to grapple with. They are hard because we have to look at ourselves and see what is actually happening.

REMEMBER THE PRODIGAL SON

Let's remind ourselves of the story Jesus told about the prodigal son. The son had chosen to leave behind his sonship. He had asked for his father to be like a dead man, and taken the inheritance. He had chosen to separate himself from his father, who loved him, and go off to squander all he had. At the end of it, he had nothing; he had emptied himself of all he had, leaving himself poor. In his poverty he ended up with a mindset that led him to a field, caring for pigs and eating their scraps. In his poverty he realized what he had done, and that if he were to return to the father he might convince his father to take him back on as a farm boy. The son rejected the father yet concluded that he could go back, showing repentance, and receive something. The boy failed to realize who he was. In his poverty, he stripped himself of his real identity.

Sonship.

The boy made himself a pauper, but his real identity was that of a son. He needed a mind-shift. But even if the boy didn't get it, his father certainly did, and that's why he robed him, ringed him, and put shoes on his feet. The boy's identity was not changed, even if the boy failed to see it himself.

What do we learn from the story of the prodigal son? We learn that we are children of the Father. We are sons and daughters of the Father, who is the King.

The story is about us, and is actually a story of prodigal princes and prodigal princesses.

We are part of the royal family.

We are not paupers, but princesses and princes.

ROYAL CHILDREN

Royal children don't see themselves as victims; they see themselves as blessed. They see themselves as people others want to be with, to trust, and to accept. Royal children know who they are and whose ear they have. They know they can turn to the king or queen and seek their guidance. They can go to places under the royal crest and present the views of the king or queen.

Royal children realize they have power and authority because of their bloodline.

Have you ever thought about how the royal family address the Queen? If you or I were to approach the Queen, we would have to address her as "Your Majesty". But what about Princes William and Harry, or even her great-grandson George? Prince Harry was seen shouting, "Go, Granny," when the Queen "parachuted" into the opening ceremony of the Olympic Games in 2012 in a James Bond-themed stunt. When asked about it, he simply said, "To me she's just Granny." He has the authority to call her by a different name because of who he is.

Harry calls her "Granny".

The prodigal prince calls Him Father.

You have the position of a child of God. You are in the bloodline. You get to do the same. You get to call the King Father, Abba, Daddy.

I want to take this to the next step. It's not just the authority over what you call God; it's also about what you do in His name.

VIP PASS/BAR TAB

A few years ago I joined the leadership team of Spring Harvest. Spring Harvest is a large Christian conference in the UK that meets every Easter. I've been going for many years, first as someone who attended, then as a steward. I've been involved in the youth work and the adult speaker team. Some years back I was invited to join the planning group for the conference. It was and is a massive privilege to be on the team of a conference with such longevity. When I arrived at the event for the first time with this new responsibility, I was given a package with my room key and prayer ministry badge. On top of this were two other things. First, my lanyard, which had a yellow pass attached to it. It was a card with my picture on it and the letters "ELT": Event Leadership Team. This yellow ELT badge meant I had an all-access pass. I could go anywhere. I had been given the authority to go wherever I needed. Secondly, I had a Bar Tab card. I had the authority to buy drinks at the after-hours bar.

I stopped.

I couldn't believe it.

They trusted me.

"I've got authority. No way!" I thought.

I could use the Spring Harvest all-access pass. I could go anywhere and buy anyone a drink. I had been given authority.

Not only that; with this pass I was Spring Harvest. The yellow pass told people I was Spring Harvest. This meant they weren't interested in where I could go or what venues I could access; they were interested that I could be approached to solve their problems.

I am Spring Harvest. I don't wear a badge, or carry an all-access pass, but I am Spring Harvest. The pass made me realize that, but I didn't need it. The pass didn't give me authority: I had already received that the moment I joined the team.

It still makes me smile that I am trusted in this way.

THE TWO GUYS LOOKED DODGE

Many years ago, when I was a youth worker, I and some colleagues were running a small music and arts festival in our local park. We had been running it for a number of years and had seen the crowd grow over that time. During one of my "walk-arounds", I spotted two guys on the edge, watching the festival. It was a public space so they had every right to be there, but there was something about them I didn't like. We kept our eye on them, and we saw them waving kids over and inviting them to take something from them. We realized they were selling something – possibly drugs – and we needed to do something about it.

Let me explain something about these two men. They were six feet tall, built like terminators, and stood with real bravado. They certainly weren't incognito, and I was not willing to approach them on my own in fear of what they might do. Knowing we needed to do something, we called the police and asked them to come and do something about these guys.

A short time passed and we saw a police car pull into the park not far from the two Arnold Schwarzeneggers. The car door opened and out stepped a young policewoman and her partner. Neither looked any more than five feet tall. She was smaller than her partner, and my heart sank. I had images of them walking over to the two men and being ignored. I had images of the two officers making a swing at them and it not making the slightest difference, or of them hanging on to the two men's legs as they simply walked away. There was little that I thought these two could do.

How wrong I was. In the blink of an eye, the short female officer had them up against the side of the police car. She didn't look much, but she had the moves. She had the Metropolitan Police uniform with its badge, and with it she had the power, authority, and commission to be the law.

You are clothed in Christ and are given an authority pass. Do you believe this? Remember what Jesus said to His disciples:

> *Then Jesus came to them and said, "All authority in heaven and on earth has been given to me."*

Matthew 28:18

> *"I will give you the keys of the kingdom of heaven; whatever you bind on earth will be*

bound in heaven, and whatever you loose on
earth will be loosed in heaven."

Matthew 16:19

The One with authority has given you the authority of the
kingdom. This authority is something that needs to be given
by Him, but it is also something we need to take. Unless we
take the authority, we miss out on what the Father has for us.
Sadly, we as the church have missed this opportunity for far
too long. Rather than being the people He longs for us to be,
we see Him as a cosmic vending machine. We come to Him
in prayer, asking for what we want to see happen, while at the
same time He's saying back to us, "I've given you authority to
bind and loose on earth." We paralyze ourselves by not taking
what is given to us.

LONG JOURNEY

Jesus told a story about exactly this. In Mark 13:34–37 He
told the disciples a story about authority. The story is one that
we live each day and still fail to see the significance of.

There was once a man who owned some land and a lovely
estate house. He was a man of significance and authority. He
was so wealthy that he had servants who ran the house for him.
Before he embarked on a long journey he turned to his servants
and put them in charge of the house and the estate. He gave
each their own task in caring for the property and told one of
them to keep watch for his return. He wanted to make sure they
would be ready for him on his return. He didn't want to find the
light out and the heating off if he were to return at night.

This man gave his servants the rule of the property. They were to govern what he had, to protect his assets and see the gardens grow and flourish. They weren't to close everything down, putting dust covers over the furniture, but they were to keep the house alive. They had authority to make necessary decisions in the way that the master would do if he were there himself.

The situation is this: Jesus has gone but He has left us with authority over His house. We are given the authority to do His kingdom work and to care for His home, planet Earth.

Imagine if the master had returned to find that the servants had done nothing. The rooms were dusty, they hadn't opened the post, bills had not been paid. Everything was left as it was when he went away, but because they had done nothing the paintwork had flaked, the grass had become overgrown, and the flowerbeds hadn't been weeded. When they were asked why they had done nothing, they said, "You didn't tell us you wanted us to do it."

The master would look confused and say, "I gave you the keys to the house. I gave you authority over the estate accounts to pay for work to be done."

The servants would respond, "But you didn't tell us what to do each day."

The Master doesn't need to keep telling you what to do; He has already done that. He has given the servants the keys and the authority. There is nothing more we need to do other than to accept it and get on with it.

So what kind of authority are we given, and what does it look like in practice?

WHAT KIND OF AUTHORITY DO WE HAVE?

We have two kinds of authority: one over creation and one over the reality within creation. In the final section of this book, let's unpack what this authority looks like and how it works.

RADA

The book of Genesis starts by telling us who we are and why we are. Genesis 1:26–27 (NRSVA) reads:

> Then God said, "Let us make humankind in our image, according to our likeness; let them have dominion [Hebrew rada, meaning 'authority'] over the fish of the sea, and over the birds of the air, and over the cattle, and over all the wild animals of the earth, and over every creeping thing that creeps on the earth."

We were created in His likeness, and we were given authority over the rest of creation. Adam and Eve were given authority to manage all matters on the earth. God gave them the authority to care for His property and estate in His absence. This authority was to bring justice to the earth, not to consume as dictators but to be liberators, life-givers, and creators.

Adam and Eve, and we today, are to leave planet Earth in a better state under our authority than when we found it. This means we should care about the planet and the creation within it. It means we have been given authority to make sure the garden is in a better state from one generation to the next. It means we care about the planet even if others don't.

EXUSIA

In Luke 9:1–6 we see Jesus gather His disciples together and give them exactly what they needed for the work ahead.

> When Jesus had called the Twelve together, he gave them power [Greek dunamis, from which we get the word 'dynamite') and authority (Greek exusia) to drive out all demons and to cure diseases, and he sent them out to proclaim the kingdom of God and to heal those who were ill. He told them: "Take nothing for the journey – no staff, no bag, no bread, no money, no extra shirt. Whatever house you enter, stay there until you leave that town. If people do not welcome you, leave their town and shake the dust off your feet as a testimony against them." So they set out and went from village to village, proclaiming the good news and healing people everywhere.

The word used here for authority is the Greek word *exusia*. It's a deep, rich, powerful word, directly linked to a supernatural power and authority. It would often be used by the caesar when talking about his authority, because the caesar wanted to connect himself with divine power and authority. If his authority was human, it would give him some power, humanly speaking, but he wanted ultimate power. The Romans talked about having *exusia* on a military front. They believed they had a supernatural authority in battle and that when they fought they would do so with the gods behind them.

This Greek word originated from another root word; one with which it was connected or strongly associated. *Exusia* originally came from the word *thronos*, from which we get the word "throne".

Another way of looking at this is that God's *exusia* comes when He gives His throne away. Think about that in terms of giving His throne away to His children. We are told that Jesus is seated at the right hand of the Father. Jesus is seated with the Father, both on royal thrones, and now He shares his authority with us.

According to Luke 9, His authority is given to:

Drive out demons and cure diseases;

Proclaim the kingdom;

Heal the sick.

In other words, His authority given to us allows us to drive away; it gives us the right to proclaim with power and to announce a new reality. This means we have the authority to tell all kinds of demonic beings and manifestations to head back to hell. We have the authority to speak Jesus' good news and make it our good news. We have the authority to pronounce healing over the sick. It means that our all-areas authority pass is all we need to tell demons to run, to announce freedom and salvation, and to pronounce healing.

We have this authority. As 2 Timothy 1:7 puts it, we have no need to be timid if we are walking in His power, love, and self-discipline.

EXPECTATION LINE

Let me ask you this question: have you been living below the expectation line of Jesus?

I was chatting with a guy in a coffee shop some time ago and we got talking about funding applications. He was telling me he had applied for half a million pounds for help with his local charity work. He spent time filling the form in, making sure he hit all the criteria; he asked friends to read it and reread it. He posted the form off in a crisp envelope and made sure it arrived on the grant-maker's desk in good time.

A few weeks later he received a reply to his application. The letter simply read: "We are not interested in applications below a million pounds. Please revisit your application and reapply when you have a project needing this level of funding."

Imagine that! He was told he couldn't have the money because his request was well below the line of what they offered. Essentially, he was told to go back and dream up a plan for a million pounds.

His application was below the expectation line. Do we do the same? Are we living below the expectation line of what is possible with God?

A TESTIMONY OF AUTHORITY

I have a friend, whom we will call Sarah, who found herself sat around a dinner table with a group of women of another faith. One of them, whom we will call Clara, was struggling with a headache and dizziness. During a pause in the meal, Sarah leant over and offered to pray the migraine away. Going to another room with an unsure Clara, Sarah prayed with authority for the pain to go away. Within a moment the woman was well, the pain had gone, and she was no longer feeling dizzy.

A month passed and Sarah found herself once again around the dinner table with Clara and another one of her friends. During the meal, Clara turned to her friend and encouraged her to tell Sarah about her struggle with depression. The friend explained to Sarah about how depression had taken over her life and mind, and about how she felt hopeless and suicidal. Clara asked Sarah if she could pray again to her God. Sarah wasn't sure. Depression was a much bigger issue than a headache. Nevertheless, Sarah agreed to pray, believing that if she wasn't healed God would show His love to the woman in the prayer anyway. Sarah prayed again with authority and pronounced healing. The woman thanked her and they finished the meal, and Sarah hoped and prayed that the woman might have sensed something of God's love.

Months passed, and Sarah was at home one day when the doorbell rang. It was the woman with depression, but this time she looked significantly different. She looked lighter and brighter. The woman told Sarah she had left that day feeling different and that the depression had lifted. She no longer felt suicidal and thanked Sarah for praying.

Sarah was gobsmacked. Her expectation had been that little would happen, but Jesus' expectation was huge.

Are we applying for half a million when the King has a much bigger bank account for us to draw from?

A DELEGATED AUTHORITY

So what is it that God knows about us? He knows we have authority because He has authority. The authority we enjoy is a delegated authority.

We could say it like this: we are the executors of Jesus' kingdom will. We have authority over what He has authority over. He has given us the power to do what He would be doing. This is all possible because He has given us the keys to the kingdom, the family credit card, and the family signature.

Yet with all this in mind, we might still say, "But I'm not able or capable." We still believe we can't, or that we don't have the authority.

Imagine that moment in Jerusalem when Jesus rides into the city on a donkey. People are screaming and cheering. People are mobbing and reaching out to touch Jesus. Imagine the scene from the donkey's perspective. Imagine him telling his donkey friends, "Do you remember when I walked that day into Jerusalem, and all the people put their garments and palm branches in the way and cried 'Hosanna'?" The other donkeys would be shocked: how had he made it about him?

The reality is we are more likely to do the opposite. Imagine this scene for a moment: the donkey is carrying Jesus, and people are cheering "Hosanna" and placing their coats on the floor. Then imagine the donkey speaking up: "It's not me! It's not me! I'm nobody." That would only have revealed the donkey's arrogance. No one was praising the donkey; they were praising the One who was riding the donkey.

The donkey was only the vehicle of Jesus.

I have to constantly remind myself we are just the ass carrying Jesus, and I can guarantee you will not find a bigger ass than me.

What is it that God knows? He knows that we have authority because we carry Jesus.

A WARNING ABOUT AUTHORITY

I do have a couple of clear warnings around authority. The authority that we are given does not make us superior. Sometimes, when we are given a little bit of authority, we can allow it to grow and become something it's not. Authority is not power over others, but more a power to do, to live, and to empower others. We aren't superior because we carry Jesus' VIP pass; in fact, the opposite is the truth. We are servants who are given the authority of the Master. We aren't given His authority to rule over people but to be like Christ to them.

What does Jesus' authority look like? Well, it looks like commanding demons to flee, it looks like pronouncing resurrection, healing, and restoration. It is also an authority that looks like bending the knee with a towel around our waist and washing others' feet. Jesus had authority over all things, yet He did not cling to the power, but instead He used it to serve and love others. He used it to honour and empower and bless people.

A number of years ago I worked in an office where there was an administrator for the organization. The administrator had little authority in other areas of his life, and the office became his little empire. Staplers had labels on and stationery cupboards were locked and not opened unless he was available to open them. He used his power to rule over others in the office rather than enabling others to be and to do the best they could in the workplace. He used the power to make himself indispensable. Do you know anyone like that?

Maybe you see a little of that in yourself.

We can do this all the time without realizing it.

The truth is, we don't need this kind of authority over people. Jesus' authority was lived out washing feet, feeding people, and dying on a cross. Jesus' authority came through His subversive actions.

My other point is this: authority is not a perk but a serious responsibility. We are given authority to do the work of the kingdom. The authority is not for our benefit but for the benefit of the kingdom.

Jesus gives us keys to the kingdom, His bank account PIN, and His royal ring. This is a serious responsibility. Will we squander the responsibility or will we use it? Will we let it go to waste or will we be proactive?

Remember the story Jesus told in Matthew 25:14–30. A rich man gives to his servants some finance and the authority to do something with it. To the first servant he gives five talents – a large sum of money. To the second he gives two talents, and to the third one talent. On the man's return, he asks his servants to show what they have done with the talents and the authority he has given them. Two of the servants have earned a 100 per cent return on the money by trading with the funds. The third servant returns to his master and reveals that he hid the money in the ground for safekeeping and it has earned nothing in return. So the two who have done something are rewarded, but the third, who has neglected the authority he was given, is severely punished.

The story is meant to challenge us to look at what we are given and to ask whether we are using it well or wasting what we have in our hands.

What is it God knows about you? He knows He has given you His authority. Using the analogy of the story, He has gone on a journey and left you with the care of His property and the authority to do something with it in His name. The question is, what are you going to do?

God is giving you His authority and He wants you to run with it and explore it. He wants you to dream, to share Jesus, to act in His name, to pray with authority. He's doing this to allow us to give things a go, to make mistakes. He's giving us authority to question and authority to do what Jesus did.

EPILOGUE

There are two great days in a person's life – the day we are born and the day we discover why.
William Barclay

We started this book with the story of Rabbi Akiva. Rabbi Akiva stood at the gates of the Roman garrison and the centurion shouted down to him: "Who are you? What are you doing here?"

Why would a rabbi like Akiva be willing to pay twice the amount of the Roman centurion's wage simply for him to ask him two questions each morning?

It tells us that these two questions are foundational to who we are, and that they are questions Rabbi Akiva was already asking himself. It was simply that someone had articulated the challenge.

The two questions focus us clearly on first our "identity" and then our "purpose".

Who are you? This isn't a question about what your name is, but is rather a question about who you really are beyond that. Who are you when the lights go out? Who are you when everything is stripped away from you? In the pages of this book we have explored the "Who are you?" question. You are a son or daughter. You are a son or daughter who has wandered away, but you are also a son or daughter who is no longer an orphan but an adopted child of the most high God. You have been welcomed home, a robe has been placed on your back, a ring on your finger, and shoes on your feet. You are royalty in the household of the King. You are a child who is created in the very reflection of your divine Father. The Bible reveals that you are created in the image and likeness of this Father, who placed His creativity and ability within each cell of your body.

What are you doing here? The Roman wanted to know why Akiva was trespassing. But we are asked the same question today. What are we doing here? What we are doing comes out of who we are. If we are royal sons and daughters placed within this time and place in human history, then we have to ask: what is the plan? Because of your identity there is an activity.

Do you remember why Rabbi Akiva lost his way that day? He was meditating on Isaiah 43. He was asking a question about his purpose:

> *"But you are my witnesses, O Israel!" says*
> *the Lord. "You are my servant. You have*
> *been chosen to know me, believe in me, and*
> *understand that I alone am God.*
> *There is no other God –*
> * there never has been, and there never will be.*
> *I, yes I, am the Lord,*
> * and there is no other Savior."*

Isaiah 43:10–11 (NLT)

Why are we here? We are here to be sons and daughters who witness to and serve our Father. We have been given the power and authority to do His work and represent Him to the world. We have been given the gifts of the kingdom to do the family work.

What is the family work? Creating, making, reshaping, restoring, resurrecting, and repairing. The family work is the resurrection: resurrection of people, places, broken arms and broken lives, broken neighbourhoods and broken neighbours. We are here to be people of the resurrection, to be restorers of broken places.

What if we knew what God knows about us? He knows we are family and we are to do His family work. He knows that we aren't meant to be lost, confused, and uncertain, but rather children who manoeuvre with the identity we have rooted in Him. He knows that He has given His keys of the kingdom to us, along with the authority to use them for His resurrection work.

So I want to end this book by asking those two questions. But this time you have to answer them:

Who are you?

Why are you here?

Are you going to continue to be unclear about who you are and what gives you your identity? Are you going to try to find other things to fill that gap within your soul? Or are you going to accept that it's not about what you can do but it's about what He has done for you.

And are you going to continue to be unclear in what your task is? Are you going to find other things to fill your time? Or are you going to accept the power designated to you, with the authority you carry, and get on doing the Father's work, practising resurrection?

How much would you be willing to pay to have someone ask you those two questions every morning?

For me, it's priceless.

SEVEN DAY ACTION PLAN

We have come full circle. Rather than rushing on to the next thing, let's take some time to wait on God to see what He says and to ask Him to reveal His plans for us. This book navigates seven chapters, and now we are going to navigate seven days: one week to allow the contents to take root within us and bring about change. Remember, this isn't about knowing more; it's about knowing Him more and allowing Him to have control.

On each of the coming seven days we will meditate upon a passage of Scripture, give ourselves something to do, and pray a prayer. This is not a tick-the-box exercise, and the more you give to allowing the concepts to marinate within you, the more you will get from it.

Why are we doing this? There is so much at stake when we as the church don't walk in the power and authority we are given. Within this book we have looked at our position, the promises made to us, and the authority we are given. But the danger is that these pages will stay as ideas rather than being the runway to allow us to take off. The following seven days are about giving us the momentum to make reality what is actually already true but unrealized.

[DAY 1]
WHAT WE KNOW
GOVERNS WHAT
WE DO

READING

This is what the Lord says –
He who made you, who formed you in the womb,
and who will help you:
Do not be afraid.

Isaiah 44:2

THOUGHT

Your life is not an accident or a mistake. For some it may be true that our parents did not deliberately plan us, but we are all alive because God wants us to be alive.

We start this week by recognizing that your life was first set into motion because He wanted you to exist. He made you in your mother's womb before anyone else knew of your existence. This isn't a message just for you; it's a message for the world. When you see people more and more as made in His image, as God's handiwork, it should raise the value you hold for your fellow human beings.

Start the day with a renewed attitude. Your position and location in the world is not an accident. Your life was designed, and so was the rest of humanity. Accidents are "God-incidents", which means you are to walk into the day with a sense of purpose and appreciation.

> I praise you because I am fearfully and
>   wonderfully made;
>   your works are wonderful,
>   I know that full well.

Psalm 139:14

How does this change the way you see yourself?

How does this change the way you see your day ahead?

How will your day become an act of praise because you are wonderfully made?

What you know about yourself will govern how you move through the day. If you think you are a mistake, you will keep apologizing for existing. If you think you have no value, you will think your opinions have no worth. Remember you were created to be amazing and to represent your Father in all you do.

TO DO

Ask God to tell you something about yourself that you need to hear.

Pick someone you will be seeing today and ask God what He is saying to you for them. Could you think about sharing this with them? If nothing else, could you share with someone else that they too are fearfully and wonderfully made?

PRAYER

Father,

May nothing other than Your view and reality of me determine my actions today. May I only make choices from Your understanding of my position.

May I not act from fear but from gratitude and thanksgiving. You know everything about me; show me today what You know.

Amen.

[DAY 2] WE ARE SONS AND DAUGHTERS

READING

> *"I will not leave you as orphans; I will come to you."*

John 14:18

THOUGHT

You have a position in the world: it's the position of a son or daughter. Through faith, you have been adopted into the family, which means you wear the family clothing. This clothing sets you apart from others who don't wear it. As you walk into the office, school playground, coffee shop, bank, you do so as a royal child. This doesn't give you superiority but a leadership position. Your adopted role in the world gives you authority to represent your Father as an ambassador.

> *"We are therefore Christ's ambassadors, as though God were making his appeal through us. We implore you on Christ's behalf: be reconciled to God."*

2 Corinthians 5:20

Therefore you speak for Him,
    you act for Him
    and you serve like Him.

You represent the family in all family business. You speak, act, and serve as a member of this family. As you set out on a new day, what does this look like for you? How are your words going to be His words, how are you going to act like Him, and how are you going to serve like Him?

To be ambassadors, we have to surrender to the will of the One we represent. We can't be an ambassador and promote our own way.

TO DO

Take a moment to position yourself in Jesus. Imagine standing before the Father in His throne room. You are wearing Jesus' robe: a sinner, forgiven by grace, wearing Jesus' resurrection garment. Your primary identity now is not that of sinner but that of son or daughter. You are clothed in royal robes. The Father reaches out and blesses you. Allow the Father to reach out and place His hand on your head. Hear His words.

Take a moment to receive these words as a response:

> *He redeemed us in order that the blessing given to Abraham might come to the Gentiles through Christ Jesus, so that by faith we might receive the promise of the Spirit.*

Galatians 3:14

Intentionally journey through today, knowing your heavenly position and that you have received the Holy Spirit. Because of this, look for opportunities to *speak*, *act*, and *serve* as your Father. Be His hands and feet in the world. Is there one person today you can love as Jesus loved?

PRAYER

Father,

Thank You that You love me and have adopted me as Your child.

Thank You for my position in the family.

May I now trust You that I am safe and secure, with nothing to prove for Your love.

Amen.

[DAY 3] WE ARE BEAUTIFULLY WEIRD

READING

> But you are a chosen people, a royal priesthood,
> a holy nation, God's special possession, that you
> may declare the praises of him who called you
> out of darkness into his wonderful light.

1 Peter 2:9

THOUGHT

Not only do you have a position, but you also have influence.
Today we are going to accept our kingdom influence. If
the Queen were to walk into the room, people would act
differently because of her influence. The same is true of
Jesus. When Jesus walked into a room, He would have an
impact on the atmosphere. Something about His holiness
would transform the space around Him. When Jesus changes
us, we become a holy people, a holy antiseptic in the world.
This means that when we enter a place, our very nature
should change the atmosphere beautifully. It should be
noticeable that people of the resurrection are in the room.

Reconciliation should happen, peace should be made, and love should be shared.

Make a conscious decision to be beautifully weird today. Make a decision to bring about something holy and pleasing in your workplace, neighbourhood, or home. Be a person of Jesus' influence. Imagine wearing the aroma of Christ: how would such a beautiful perfume influence the room?

If you can't imagine how your presence could make a difference, start by choosing to live differently.

TO DO

Practise these five life hacks today:
1. Have an attitude of gratitude.
2. Stay away from gossip.
3. Praise people and say thank you.
4. Choose to be diplomatic and respectful.
5. Be honest and loving.

Offer this way of life to Jesus as a start of this process of having a kingdom influence.

PRAYER

Father,

Jesus walked into the room and darkness trembled.

Fill me with light that I might do the same.

May I receive Your holiness today so that I might be a holy antiseptic.

May my actions create community, pronounce new life, and reveal Your kingdom.

May my life be the home of Your Spirit, that His work in me might bring about radical change in each room, journey, and interaction.

May my life have influence beyond what can be seen.

May I be Your holy presence in the most normal of places.

Amen.

[DAY 4]
WE ARE
POWERFUL

READING

> *"Truly I tell you, if you have faith as small as a mustard seed, you can say to this mountain, 'Move from here to there,' and it will move. Nothing will be impossible for you."*

Matthew 17:20

THOUGHT

Jesus wants us to be the kind of people who, each morning when our feet hit the floor, the devil says, "Oh no, they're up."

Because of who you are and Whose you are, the devil has nothing on you. All he is going to try to do is undermine your position, because with position comes influence and power. You are far more powerful than you recognize because of your position in the family and the influence you have.

Jesus knows how powerful your prayers are, how powerful your commands are, and how powerful your pronouncements are. Jesus says that you can tell mountains to move and they will: mountains made of stone, mountains made of fear, and mountains made of sickness.

The results of prayer are not linked to the person praying. Prayer is powerful, even when the person praying doesn't realize it. The power is always God's, which He shares with us when we pray. He gives us authority to pray in the name of Jesus and to command things to happen in His name. We are told in 1 John 5:14–15:

> *This is the confidence we have in approaching God: that if we ask anything according to his will, he hears us. And if we know that he hears us – whatever we ask – we know that we have what we asked of him.*

You might pray with passion, clarity, and educated language, or you might pray with a whisper and poor diction. Prayer isn't determined by *your* ability, but by *His* ability. God is simply looking for our availability.

TO DO

Make yourself available today to pray for someone you know who needs change in their life, be it healing, hope, or new opportunities. You might find it helpful to take a moment to listen to God and see if He shares with you someone to be praying for or an opportunity to pray into. He may give you something specific that He wants to do; all you have to do then is find who that's for.

PRAYER

Father,

Thank You that, through Your adoption, I have all that I need today to get through what is before me. You have given me authority to pray in Your Son's name and have empowered me by Your Holy Spirit. Thank You that I can now participate in Your divine nature because of Jesus.

Fill me now with Your Spirit, that by Him, in the practical events of today, I would be wise and careful.

Thank You that by Your power I can pray for the sick, pronounce healing, and restore relationships. Give me opportunities to not just believe it but also to live it.

Amen.

[DAY 5]
WE ARE ABLE
AND CAPABLE

READING

*His divine power has given us everything we
need for a godly life through our knowledge
of him who called us by his own glory and
goodness. Through these he has given us
his very great and precious promises, so that
through them you may participate in the divine
nature, having escaped the corruption in the
world caused by evil desires.*

2 Peter 1:3–4

THOUGHT

Your Father in His wisdom has given you everything you
need. To believe anything else is to believe our Father is a
liar. As you look out over the day ahead, there is nothing
that you can't handle or deal with, because He has given you
everything. It may be that in the moment you come up against
trouble, you will receive what you need. The moment before
you haven't got what it takes, but by trusting in Him, in that

moment you have it. You are able and capable of facing what is ahead because He has positioned you with family status, given you family influence and power. The only way you will not be able and capable is if you choose not to believe this. The danger is that we will allow fear to rule our day, and so choose to be powerless over the events that unfold.

Take a moment to breathe in. Remind yourself that in yourself you don't have what is needed, and then allow yourself to speak the words, "But Jesus does."

We have to be able to say, "I am not good enough, BUT Jesus is."

Your day is mapped out with three truths: 1) You may not have what it takes; 2) but you are enough in Him; and 3) Jesus does have what it takes.

TO DO

Make a conscious effort to give yourself time to look for opportunities to pray for people and hear words of encouragement for them. Be courageous and share what you hear God say. If nothing else, even if you hear something wrong, people will know you are praying for them and feel the love.

It is worth noting, if you haven't done so before, that prayer for others should be encouraging and uplifting. In the sharing of prophetic words we don't allow people to share words that could potentially hurt someone, so we ask them to avoid birthdays, deaths, and marriages. They can share these with the team so we can pray about them. This is helpful so as not to raise people's hopes in an unhelpful way. We should only use encouraging and positive words to bless those we are praying for, and we definitely should not make promises in our prayers.

PRAYER

Father, without You I am nothing.
Without Your breath of life, I would still be but dust.
Thank You for Your power, life, and energy.
I choose to stand in You today and to recognize that in You I
am all I need to be.

Amen.

[DAY 6]
WE ARE
GIFTED

READING

*We have different gifts, according to the grace
[God's generosity] given to each of us. If your
gift is prophesying, then prophesy in accordance
with your faith; if it is serving, then serve; if it is
teaching, then teach; if it is to encourage, then
give encouragement; if it is giving, then give
generously; if it is to lead, do it diligently; if it is
to show mercy, do it cheerfully.*

Romans 12:6–8

THOUGHT

We are told in the Bible, "God is love" (1 John 4:8). This love
at the heart of who He is affects all the ways He relates to
us and how He behaves. Creation itself was an act of love.
God has revealed Himself as a generous creator, a generous
saviour, and a generous giver. God has generously given
good gifts to His children, each one having the family gifts
available but also needing to recognize that He has gifted

each of us with special gifts that fit our passions, character, and needs.

All of God's children are in the "gifted and talented" pool. No one is left on the outside looking in; we each have what is needed.

In Chapter 6 we talked about the two barriers that will stop us from doing what we were made to do: wrong comparison and the fear of failure.

If you set out on the day ahead comparing yourself to others, you will always lose. You will end up depressed, anxious, and unwilling to give things a go. If you allow fear of failure to determine your day, you will not try anything new; you will only do what has always been done.

It is often said that if we only do what we have always done, we will inevitably get the same results we have always got before.

TO DO

Earlier in the book we talked about the characteristics of orphans. Comparison is one of them. You are not an orphan; you are a son or daughter, which mean there is no need to compare yourself. The only person comparison will destroy is yourself; it will lead to the fear of getting things wrong. Our biggest gift to breaking the rod of comparison is actually failing. When we start to fail and we even celebrate failure, we no longer play into the fear of comparison. If you keep thinking failure is just failure, you will always place yourself in the failure bin. But the truth is, any risk-taking is a win. Putting yourself out there is a win. You will become successful because you dared to fail.

I want to challenge you today to fail, often and quickly. Our tendency is to try to cling to dignity rather than God. Failure means we put down dignity and allow ourselves to cling to God.

Take every opportunity to pray over someone for healing at every opportunity. If they tell you they don't want prayer – WIN. You risked and you won. If you pray and nothing happens – WIN. You risked and you won. Breaking the rod of fear and comparison will only happen when we celebrate failure and risk-taking.

Remember, we are drawn toward safety, but we were made for adventure. The devil wants us to choose a no-risk future.

PRAYER

Father,

More often than not we are motivated by fear rather than the possible gain.

I have made safety the win, but I wish to change that. I want to risk everything and gain everything Your Son has for me.

May I be a risk-taker for You, not drawn to safety but to radical possibility.

Thank You that You risked everything for me. May I now live to do the same for You.

Amen.

[DAY 7]
WE ARE
AUTHORIZED

The chapters of this book have all been leading up to this point. All that the Father has done is so that you have the authority to do what He wants you to do. We were created to be God's partners; we were saved to be God's partners, and we were empowered to be God's partners. This means you have all that is needed: the position and the promises.

READING

For the spirit God gave us does not make us timid, but gives power, love and self-discipline.

2 Timothy 1:7

THOUGHT

Our biggest danger is that we will live well below the expectation line for our lives. God has commissioned us to heal the sick, proclaim the good news, and serve the poor. The danger is that we simply don't do it, because we live below the expectation line of what is possible.

Are you going to live below the expectation line of Jesus? Or are you going to make your day active and dynamic in His power and authority, and with the expectation that things will change?

TO DO

Next time you pray for someone, don't beg God to do something. Jesus tells His disciples to pray with authority. This can feel unnatural, but try praying for what is needed in the name of Jesus with the authority that has been given to you. It might be that each time you pray for something you start by saying, "I choose to remember what You have done for me in the past. I remember Your activity in my life. With the authority given to me, I pronounce... [name the thing – such as healing or freedom] over [name the person]." When we pray, we do so not as the poor begging for the scraps from the master's table. Rather, we pray as a son or daughter who has authority to tell the servants what to do in the family name. When you pray next, think about how your prayer models your authority in the family.

PRAYER

Father,

May I choose today to live up to Your expectation line for me. There have been times when I have had low expectations of You and Your kingdom. May I not allow myself to be cynical or pessimistic any longer.

With the authority You have already given me, would You give me greater opportunities to use it, greater availability to step out and try new things, and the ability to see potential for Your work.

Amen.

KEEP GOING ON THE DISCIPLESHIP ADVENTURE...

HEAD TO

wearemakingdisciples.com

AND FIND YOUR DISCIPLESHIP ASSESSMENT SHAPE WITH CRIS

A tool to be used by any church, small group or individual interested in elevating the conversation around discipleship and spiritual formation.

"Cris Rogers is the real deal: outworking his faith in the crucible of urban community as a husband and a dad, a pastor, and a friend. In this book he goes right to the heart of human identity with clarity, courage, and grace. It's a life-changing message."
Pete Greig, 24-7 Prayer International and Emmaus Rd, Guildford

"This is a must-read book for all disciples, young and old. Don't waste time; this book will change everything!"
Rob Peabody, founder of Vomo and the Awaken Movement

"Cris has the communication skills of a master storyteller combined with the insight of a wise spiritual director. Every page of this book drips with fascinating truth and wisdom, challenging us to step more fully into our God-given identity and His purposes for us. I really can't recommend it highly enough to individuals or small groups seeking spiritual growth."
Cathy Madavan, writer, speaker, coach, and author of *Digging for Diamonds* and *Living on Purpose*

"What if we knew *What God Knows About Us?* is a terrific read. The powerful reminder that who we are in Christ shapes our identity, purpose, place, and significance is vital in a society that devalues people so often, or gives us worth because of what we have or what we do.

With the skilful eye of a good theologian and the loving heart of a pastor, Cris Rogers tells us a better story about ourselves. He draws us back to the reality of who we are in Christ and helps us understand that what God has done for us is the fundamental building block of a life well lived.

If you or someone you know struggles with self-image and low self-esteem then this book will help. Let its truths enable you to wipe away the dirt on the mirror of your self-understanding that have been placed there by others so you can see yourself clearly and understand how much you are loved, and how valuable and powerful you can be in God's hands."
Revd Malcolm Duncan, lead pastor, Dundonald Elim Church

"We all act according to our views of who we think we are, whether those views are accurate or not. This great book helps settle the most important questions in life, so we can get on with living it to the full."
Anthony Delaney, leader, Ivy Network

"This is a truly brilliant book. You will find it encouraging, challenging, and wonderful. It will help you be all you can in Jesus."
Gavin Calver, director for mission (England), Evangelical Alliance

Also by Cris Rogers

The Bible Book by Book (Monarch)

Practising Resurrection (Authentic)

A Monkey's Orientation (Authentic)

Naked Christianity (Kevin Mayhew)

Only the Brave (Monarch)

Making Disciples (Essential Christian)

Immeasurably More (Monarch)